Donated by

Donated By
Beverly Hoese

© DEMCO, INC. 1990 PRINTED IN U.S.A.

EL GRECO
The Burial of the Count of Orgaz

FRANCISCO CALVO SERRALLER

EL GRECO
The Burial of the Count of Orgaz

THAMES AND HUDSON

Photography by Bardazzi Fotografia, Florence

Translated from the Spanish
El Greco: El entierro del conde de Orgaz
by Jenifer Wakelyn

This edition © 1995 Thames and Hudson Ltd, London
First published in the United States of America
by Thames and Hudson, Inc.,
500 Fifth Avenue, New York, New York 10110

Copyright © 1994 Electa, Milan
Elemond Editori Associati
and Sociedad Editorial Electa España, S.A., Madrid

Library of Congress Catalog Card Number 94–61694

British Library Cataloguing-in-Publication Data

A catalogue record for this book is available
from the British Library

ISBN 0-500-23702-6

Printed and bound in Italy

Contents

The commission and its context

ON 18 MARCH 1586, when El Greco signed the contract in which he undertook to paint *The Burial of the Count of Orgaz*, he was probably 45 years of age, assuming the date of his birth in Candia, then capital of the distant island of Crete, to have been 1541. By the time of this commission he had been living in Spain for almost nine years, having arrived there in 1577 after a period in Italy. He had reached the age of physical and artistic maturity and his destiny now seemed to lie clearly before him. Well travelled, arrogant and eccentric by temperament and combative by nature, El Greco was to spend the rest of his life in Toledo, and from this time on his pictorial style would undergo no fundamental change.[1]

This date, when the contract for the monumental painting commissioned by the modest Toledan church of Santo Tomé was signed, in effect came as the culmination of many other important episodes in the artist's life. The most significant was around 1567 when he left his native Crete for Venice, where his personal and artistic ambitions underwent a transformation and he may even have become a pupil of the great Titian himself.[2] Around 1570 he moved to Rome, by all accounts ready to hazard his fortune; he took a considerable risk by daring to criticize in public Michelangelo's talent as a painter, a gamble that proved ill-fated.[3] Finally, in 1577, he came to Spain, where two distinct periods followed, each marked by very different expectations on the part of the artist. The first saw an abortive attempt to win a place at court, while during the second, having failed to gain royal approval with the *Martyrdom of St Maurice*, commissioned by Philip II and completed in 1582 for the monastery of the Escorial, he established himself in Toledo. He had already received a number of major commissions in this city, including a series of works for the church of Santo Domingo el Antiguo, and the *Espolio (Disrobing of Christ)*, painted for the cathedral, and in the 1580s he already enjoyed a considerable reputation there.

It was therefore quite natural that when Andrés Núñez of Madrid, parish priest of the church of Santo Tomé, decided to decorate the chapel containing the tomb of Don Gonzalo Ruiz of Toledo, Lord of Orgaz and a benefactor of the church, with a large canvas commemorating the legendary miracle which had immortalized the funeral obsequies of this Castilian grandee, he should turn to El Greco. At this time the artist, a parishioner of the church, lived nearby in a palatial group of buildings rented from the estates of the Marquis of Villena.

A number of dates relating to events leading up to the formal commission should also be taken into account. The first and most important of these was the successful outcome of a lawsuit brought in 1564 by the above-mentioned parish priest of Santo Tomé against the inhabitants of the town of Orgaz, who had refused to fulfil the terms of the annual endowment to the church laid down in Don Gonzalo's will. The case was settled in the plaintiff's favour by the Chancellery of Valladolid in 1569, and as a result this small, extremely modest church suddenly found itself vastly enriched. The proceeds of the case included the arrears which had accrued and must have amounted to a considerable sum.

All these circumstances are recorded, with some slight variations in the dates, in a plaque at the foot of the famous painting of *The Burial of the Count of Orgaz*. Today's visitor can still read the Latin text written as an epitaph to the dead nobleman by Dr Alvar Gómez de Castro. This inscription is of such evident interest that I quote it here in full:

Dedicated to the benefactor saints and to piety. Even if you are in haste, pause for a moment, traveller, and hear in a few words an old tale of our city. Don Gonzalo Ruiz of Toledo, Lord of the township of Orgaz, Protonotary of Castille, among other tokens of his piety made it his concern that this church of the apostle Thomas, in which he desired to be buried, but which was formerly meagre and impoverished, should be restored and enlarged at his expense; and he made many offerings, both in silver and in gold. When the priests were preparing to bury him — wonderful and extraordinary to behold! — St Stephen and St Augustine descended from heaven and buried him here with their own hands. As it would take a long time to explain why these saints did this, enquire of the holy brothers of St Augustine, if you have time. The way is short. He died in the year of Our Lord 1312. You have heard the gratitude of those who dwell in heaven. Now hearken to the inconstancy of mortals. The said Gonzalo bequeathed to the parish priest and the ministers of this church and to the poor of the parish 2 sheep, 16 hens, 2 skins of wine, 2 wagon loads of wood and 800 coins which we call *maravedis*, all to fall due each year from the inhabitants of the domain of Orgaz. For two years they refused to pay this pious tribute, hoping that with the passage of time their obligation would be forgotten. It was enforced by order of the Chancellery of Valladolid in the year of Our Lord 1570, the case having been energetically pleaded by Andrés Núñez of Madrid, priest of this church, and the steward, Pedro Ruiz Durón.[4]

This text in fact imparts most of the relevant information about the miracle which the painting commemorates and also about the events which made the commission possible, that is to say, the proceeds of the lawsuit. Clearly, in addition to the zeal for which he is praised in the epitaph and the boldness required to bring the lawsuit in the first place (the Spanish curse, *¡Dios te dé pleitos y los ganes!* [May God send you lawsuits and you win them!] is still current today), the parish priest of Santo Tomé must have been endowed with the practical virtues of perseverance and determination. These qualities are certainly evinced in the skilful plan drawn up by Andrés Núñez for improvements to the church and for a memorial in honour of Don Gonzalo Ruiz. The nature of the supernatural event by which he chose to commemorate the dead benefactor meant that he not only had to decide on the artist best qualified to undertake the commission, but first and foremost he had to obtain episcopal approval for this mysterious miracle to be celebrated in paint. Indeed, the miracle was so enigmatic and arcane that it is more than likely that, had El Greco's painting not been commissioned, it would have become just one more of the many legendary and supernatural occurrences which have gradually fallen into complete oblivion.

In 1583, then, Andrés Núñez successfully obtained, firstly, official recognition of the miracle and, secondly, as required by the relevant rulings of the Council of Trent,[5] episcopal authorization for it to be depicted in a painting. All this was done, as we shall see, two years before El Greco was formally contracted to take on the commission.

However, before we go on to examinine the terms of the contract, which were not restricted to financial arrange-ments, let us pause for a moment to take a closer look at Don Gonzalo Ruiz of Toledo, Lord of Orgaz. The miracle which transpired during his funeral was now, some 250 years later, being celebrated; even after this lapse of time, the church of Santo Tomé was still able to depend on the generous terms of his bequest. The date given in the epitaph must first be corrected; the Lord of Orgaz actually died in 1323, and the miraculous event with which he was favoured occurred in 1327, when his remains were transferred from the monastery of St Augustine to Santo Tomé.

Manuel Bartolomé Cossío brought together and published in 1908 a transcription of all the extant descriptions of the charitable nobleman and of the miraculous event which made him famous.[6] Cossío followed the account given in Francisco de Pisa's 1612 manuscript of the *Apuntamientos*,[7] itself taken from the 1588 Toledo edition of the *Extravagantes* by Alonso de Villegas,[8] and collated it with other relevant sources, such as the history of Toledo by Pedro Alcocer[9] and the *Crónicas de la Orden de San Agustín*. Thus we are informed that Don Gonzalo Ruiz of Toledo, 'a direct descendant of Don Esteban Illán, himself descended from Don Pedro Paleólogo, third son of the Emperor of Constantinople (whose descendants include the dukes of Alba and the counts of Oropesa and of Orgaz)', was a native of Toledo, Lord of the town of Orgaz and Protonotary or Chancellor of Castille. (Although the title of El Greco's painting traditionally refers to the 'Count of Orgaz', this house was not in fact raised to the rank of countship until the late date of 1522.)

However, quite apart from his illustrious lineage and the privileges of his elevated position, it was his great devotion and good works which ultimately granted the noble lord a place in human and heavenly glory, since these were the qualities which were rewarded by the miracle that made his name so famous. It appears that around 1300 Don Gonzalo Ruiz ordered the church of Santo Tomé to be restored and enlarged at his expense:

In 1312 [Cossío's account continues] certain monks of the order of St Augustine who had formerly been resident, by favour of King Alfonso the Wise, in the church of St Stephen on the banks of the Tagus outside the city walls, were enabled to leave this site, which had become insalubrious. For thanks to the beneficent influence of Don Gonzalo, Queen María de Molina, wife of Sancho the Brave, allowed them to use some houses and a royal palace which she owned in Toledo. And it was the will of the Lord of Orgaz that the new church, like the one they had left, should be named after St Stephen, for which reason the glorious protomartyr and St Augustine honoured him at his burial in 1323, in the following way: the servant of God, having occupied himself during his life in performing holy works, in consequence died a saintly death. His body was taken to be buried in the church of Santo Tomé, which he had built, and being placed in the middle of the church in the presence of all the nobles of the city, when the priests had said the offices of the dead and they went to carry the body to the tomb, they saw two glorious saints, St Stephen the first martyr and St Augustine, visibly and clearly descending from on high, with faces and clothes that everyone could recognize, and reaching the body, they carried it to the tomb, where in the presence of all they placed it, saying: 'Such is the reward of those who serve God and His saints', and then they disappeared, leaving the church full of fragrance and heavenly aromas....[10]

A further note tells us that, in his will, Don Gonzalo had asked to be buried in a humble position by the west door, on the right of the entrance. This is the site of the chapel restored and enlarged centuries later by the devoted and overburdened parish priest of Santo Tomé, Andrés Núñez, who was to commission the painting from El Greco. Cossío's transcription continues:

The painting was made and it is one of the most excellent in all Spain and it cost 1,200 ducats, not including the framing. It is particularly admired by strangers who come to see it, while those of the city never tire of it but always find new things to contemplate in the painting, because it has very lifelike portraits of many famous nobles of our time. This was the work of the painter Domingo de Theotocapuli [sic], a native of Greece.[11]

This, then, is the story of the Lord of Orgaz and the reasons for his miraculous burial, which Dr Alvar Gómez de Castro described as too lengthy to explain in his epitaph.

We come next to the formal arrangements preceding the commission in which the theme to be represented by El Greco was clearly stated. Some of the stipulations in the contract, signed 18 March 1586, are of particular interest, especially those prescribing the content of the painting:

a procession showing the priest and the other divines saying the offices for the burial of Don Gonzalo ... and St Augustine and St Stephen descending to bury the body of this knight, one taking hold of his head and the other his feet, placing him in the tomb, and all around them many people watching and above all this the heavens opening in glory.[12]

However repetitive all these quotations might appear, it is, to my mind, essential to record in full the details of the icono-graphical requirements, specifying not only the figures to be portrayed, but also how they should be depicted. This latter issue was one of prime importance, sometimes leading to controversy, particularly in view of the aforementioned rulings of the Council of Trent and the general spirit of Counter-Reformation doctrine on sacred images, which was that the texts illustrated must be followed to the letter.[13] The strict prescriptions in the contract furthermore provide an indication of the conceptual framework which, together with the physical features of the painting's intended setting, predetermined the composition to be created by El Greco. We are thus enabled to gauge the extent of the painter's freedom to interpret the given theme – which was evidently extremely restricted.

Clearly then, the canvas had to give visual meaning to the story as stipulated, and this moreover on a large scale but in a constricted position on the wall of a chapel which, even when enlarged and improved, was still of modest proportions. Destined to be placed above the tomb, the painting also had to leave space below for a cartouche in which the painted epitaph was to be set. In this respect, as already mentioned, a change was made to the original arrangement, apparently without disagreement between the parties. The difficulties involved in the painting were thus considerable: the final measurements of the canvas were by no means small – it is almost five metres high and three and a half metres wide – and the top was shaped in a semicircular arch. All in all, a considerable challenge to the artist's abilities was implicit.

These factors, the scale and difficulty of the work and El Greco's brilliant resolution of the problems, as well as the reputation he enjoyed among patrons and the respect in which he was held by other artists (always much harder to earn), explain the high valuation given to the picture. It was customary for paintings to be assessed for sales tax by two expert painters, in this case Luis de Velasco and a certain Hernando from Anunciabay, near Siruelas. On the completion of the work in 1588 they valued it at the undoubtedly elevated figure of 1,200 ducats. Initially daunted by this considerable sum, the businesslike priest of Santo Tomé, without having much idea of what he was about, tried to negotiate a lower appraisal. He was then faced with a second assessment, this time made by Hernando de Ávila and Blas del Prado, who put an even higher value on the picture of 1,600 ducats.

It is not hard to imagine the effect of this new figure on the increasingly anxious priest. There then began a dispute between the two parties, as a result of which the first, initially rejected, valuation was accepted, although this agreement was not reached without some measure of reluctance on the part of the painter.

We shall dwell on this dispute for a moment, because it brings out some interesting facets of the life and personality of El Greco and also provides a more general insight into the social status of Spanish artists of this period and later. The information supplied by Gómez Moreno about the prices paid for the *Espolio* – 318 ducats – and for the *Martyrdom of St Maurice* helps to explain the significance of the disputed valuation. Although commissioned by the King himself for the royal monastery, the latter painting was valued at 800 ducats, exactly half of the second valuation of the *Burial*.[14]

This incident indicates not only that, at this point in his career, El Greco was selling his works for high prices, and that he was a staunch defender of what he saw as his rights (as was the priest of Santo Tomé, who likewise did not hesitate to seek legal redress and even to have recourse to the highest and most recondite authorities[15]), but above all it provides an illustration of the struggle in which Spanish artists were then engaged to gain more adequate recognition of the value of their work. His contemporaries certainly did not fail to acknowledge the pioneering role played by El Greco as a central figure in the struggle.[16] In this connection, for example, the writer and court painter Antonio Palomino (1653–1726), in the later but more exhaustive and systematic account of the setbacks suffered by Spanish painters of this period in their search for tangible social recognition, discussed the topic in the first volume of his monumental treatise *Museo Pictórico y Escala Óptica*:

In the second rank of nobility, of titles ratified by tribunal, the status of Painting is well accredited. The first occasion (as far as I have been able to ascertain) in which it tried its fortune, and sought justice, was when a tax official of Illescas claimed that Dominico Greco, the famous painter, should pay sales tax [*alcabala*] on the painting and sculptures for the altar of the chapel of Our Lady of Charity in the said township (even the drawing of the altar and the church are said to be by him), and having defended himself was released and absolved of the demand by the Royal Exchequer [*Real Consejo de Hacienda*]. This painting was declared exempt from taxes,

by virtue of its excellence, and this in perpetuity. This happened around 1600. And this judgment was cited in the proceedings of the next trial; and this is mentioned by Carduchi, as Butrón records, and the lawyer Ríos in his *Noticias de las Artes*.[17]

Lawsuits, disagreements and confrontations with his patrons abounded in the life of El Greco – even on occasion, as in the case described by Palomino, against the Royal Exchequer. Although scarcely surprising in view of his combative temperament, it is nevertheless significant in that El Greco became a milestone for Spanish artists in their lengthy, and indeed almost interminable, struggle for recognition and the acknowledgment of the so-called *liberalidad*, the liberal status, of painting. The implications of this status went far beyond the purely honorary in the stratified and rigidly hierarchical society of feudal Spain. In order to understand this, we should consider the various consequences, in terms of obligations to the State, of legal recognition of the liberal status of the profession: exemption both from the sales tax known as *alcabala* and from the *quinta* (a military levy), as well as from the obligation to take part in the frequent processions and numerous public activities of the guilds of the period. Furthermore, to be engaged in one of the so-called mechanical arts in principle disqualified artists from claiming noble titles and joining the ranks of the nobility; a prohibition that, as is well known, applied even to Velázquez.[18] And where contracts for commissions were concerned, to be described as belonging to a liberal rather than a mechanical profession had far-reaching consequences for the valuation of works, as is clearly illustrated by the case of El Greco's *Espolio (Disrobing of Christ)*. It was valued at 900 ducats by the expert painters, while the cathedral's assessors, basing their estimate on the criteria applied to craftsmen's works, put it at no more than 250 ducats.[19]

Manifestly then, El Greco's confrontational stance cannot simply be explained in terms of his personality, nor, as Lafuente Ferrari states in his study of conflicts over this issue in Spain during the seventeeth century, to the Spanish taste for litigation.[20] It was essentially his sound humanist education and his Italian experience that enabled El Greco to reject the anachronistic attitude then prevalent in Spain that saw the arts as mere trades.[21] Zarco del Valle's publication of documents relating to the above-mentioned lawsuit brought by El Greco against the cathedral of Toledo is most informative in this regard. Particularly revealing is the expert painters' declaration:

They declare that in their opinion, by reason of the size and the art of the Holy Scriptures of the said picture and the story it contains, its merit is so great that it is beyond price and estimation, but in view of the misery of our times and the value of such works in our day, for the work and occupation and industry and costs and time spent, 900 ducats ... [should be paid] to the said Dominico.[22]

Returning to the disputed valuation of *The Burial of the Count of Orgaz*, which did not in fact culminate in a lawsuit, it is significant that El Greco appealed to the authority of the Pope himself, a step that can justifiably be described as going to an absurd extreme. Moreover, when he finally accepted payment of the initial lower valuation of 1,200 ducats, he said he had agreed to this only 'to be done with it and to avoid lawsuits, and to spare himself further costs and expenses'.[23] In conclusion, El Greco's convictions in this regard were clearly deeply entrenched and of the utmost sincerity. Profligate and thriftless on account of his expensive and even sybaritic tastes, he constantly maintained that a painter could only become wealthy by hoarding his own works and never selling them at low prices.[24] He adhered strictly to this rule himself, and in consequence the goods listed in the inventories drawn up after his death were so meagre as almost to suggest indigence, apart from the large number of paintings that were still in his possession at the end of his life.[25]

The composition

Looking now at the history of the painting in Santo Tomé from an essentially pictorial point of view, the first topic to come under consideration is its composition. The only remaining anecdotal details of any significance are that the work took about two years to execute, from 1586 to 1588. We have already seen that, in devising the composition, El Greco adhered faithfully to the conditions made in the various clauses contained in the contract. This was to some extent in order to conform to that aspect of Counter-Reformation doctrine which, as explained above, called for 'literality' in the treatment of sacred subjects, but a great many requirements of a more fundamental nature were also invoked. These included, for example, the exaltation of acts of charity and of the fundamental role of the saints as intercessors — two issues which are at the heart of the essential theme of the *Burial*.[26]

Certainly, in the case of this painting, as of other works by El Greco, at a time when many Counter-Reformation moralists involved themselves in disputes over the precept of *decorum*, criticisms were voiced against the unseemliness of various anachronisms resulting from his approach to religious themes. Never at a loss to defend himself, his replies to these criticisms were sometimes scathing.[27] The only anachronism of which the *Burial* might be thought culpable consists in the presence of figures of the period wearing contemporary dress at an event which occurred in the past. However, the statement in Carducho's commentary on what he called '*pintura anticronismo*'[28] and '*pintura antipopeya*',[29] that 'Choices can and should be made in the way a subject is painted, as long as the fundamental essence of the event remains unchanged',[30] written several decades later in 1633 by a *dévot* completely in accord with Counter-Reformation doctrine, shows that such objections were not taken seriously. Indeed, many naturalistic effects in painting stemmed precisely from the providentialist, and hence anti-humanist, thinking of the Counter-Reformation.

Thus, in accordance with the requirements of the contract, El Greco divided his composition into two quite distinct parts. One deals with the earthly events described at length in the aforementioned clauses, and treated in detail in the picture. The other depicts celestial events, and these are represented with absolute freedom, the laconic instruction 'heavens opening in glory' leaving the interpretation of the subject to the artist's imagination. The contrast between these two parts constitutes the fundamental axis of the painting's compositional structure, and hence is at the heart of the dispute that has divided critics of almost every age up to our own, as to whether the work's status as a masterpiece in fact derives precisely from this contrast.

At all events, before we go on to analyse the artistic dialectic deployed by El Greco in his creation of an ideal synthesis between the two distinct parts of the painting, we should follow his example by first examining the available prototypes of this type of composition. By this time he had already completed a number of important commissions of equal significance and complexity, including for example the paintings for Santo Domingo el Antiguo, the *Espolio (Disrobing of Christ)*, the *Allegory of the Holy League (Dream of Philip II)*, the *Dead Christ supported by St Joseph, with the Virgin and the Magdalen (Pietá)*, and the *Martyrdom of St Maurice*. Now, with regard to these works, all the experts agree that a change of direction occurs in the *Burial* – as if, having come to terms with his failure with Philip II, El Greco had finally realized that any further attempt to try to win the favour of the Spanish with a virtuoso display of Mannerist exercises and artifices would be futile.[31]

Documentary evidence exists to show how little Philip II was drawn to the bizarre style of *St Maurice*, even though the painter had been a disciple of Titian, the artist most admired by this monarch, as also by his father Charles V. The testimony of an authoritative intermediary also informs us of the reasons for the King's disdain. I refer of course to the account written of the affair by Father Sigüenza, who dismissed the painting in the following terms:

There is a painting here by one Dominico Greco, who is now making excellent things in Toledo where he lives, of St Maurice and his soldiers, made for the particular altar of those saints. It did not please his Majesty (which is no wonder), as it found favour with few, although they say it has great art and that its author has much knowledge, and many excellent things can be seen from his hand. There are many different opinions and tastes regarding this; to me it seems that the difference between things made with good sense and with art and those made with neither is this: the former please everybody and the latter please a few, because art can only conform to what is reasonable and natural, and this is the general view, and it is thus with all paintings; something that is badly done may deceive the ignorant mind by means of certain tricks and illusions, and thus succeed in pleasing the ignorant and the thoughtless. And besides, as our own Mudo said, in his characteristic manner: *the saints must be painted in such a way that the desire to pray to them, which we may call*

devotion, is unfailing in us, because this must be the main effect and purpose of painting.[32]

I have emphasized these concluding words because, appropriately contextualized, they provide an explanation of official Spanish taste at the time.[33] We are presented here with a definitive statement of the purest and most dogmatic strand of Counter-Reformation thought, one which has led some historians to suggest that El Greco was rejected on purely moral grounds, a conclusion I consider far too simplistic. To place the views of Father Sigüenza in context, we must first note that he appealed to the authority in matters of painting of Juan Fernández Navarrete (known as El Mudo), himself also once a pupil of Titian. He is also invoked in polemic comparisons whenever the learned friar discusses in any detail the great Italian masters of late Mannerism who flocked to work on the decoration of the Escorial.[34] Thus, for example, just before he contemptuously dismisses El Greco's artistic talents, and after treating the works of some of his Italian colleagues of the period with comparable disdain, he declares:

I have mentioned only what is known of the famous artists of Italy, which is the undisputed home of painting and sculpture and where they acquired their present value, whence it has spread to Spain and to France and to other countries. Our Juan Fernández Mudo came back from there so greatly enriched that I cannot say if there was anyone who could surpass him, and those who see what he did here and compare it with the works of the great artists we have already mentioned, affirm that he was inferior to them in nothing and was superior to many. It is regrettable that what he began we might say also ended with him, as there is now no one who could even begin to compare to him.[35]

With characteristic acerbity, but now in far more intemperate language even than that employed against El Greco, Sigüenza continues the offensive, this time attacking artists of the calibre of Federico Zuccaro and Luca Cambiaso:

The other two in the palace are by the famous Federico Zuccaro; he came to replace Luca Cambiaso, just as Luca replaced El Mudo, and if the latter had lived he would have saved us from having to know so many Italians, although we would not then be so well aware of how much we had lost.[36]

I believe these extracts suffice to show that the resistance El Greco faced was something more than a trivial religious scruple, and that we should not see any artistic element in this moral attitude. It was nevertheless precisely these impulses which ultimately came to promote Spanish naturalism, as is evident from Sigüenza's emphatic defence of El Mudo. The crucial importance of *The Burial of the Count of Orgaz* within El Greco's artistic development in Spain is that in this work, as I have already argued, he appears to adapt his style to meet the incipient change in taste sweeping across the country.

Having noted this first sign of El Greco's change of artistic direction in Spain – a change of approach that in so proud a personality can hardly be described as conformity – we can now go on to explore the other sources of inspiration evinced by the composition of the painting. Here I should point out that few paintings in the entire history of art can have aroused so many and such heated disputes – although these have admittedly tended to fade away and almost disappear over time.

The first point to note is that critical interpretations of the *Burial* emphasizing its iconic background and a formal debt to Byzantine art, once part of a general trend inseparable from the Romantic fascination with an exotic image of Spain that captivated many European intellectuals and artists, now seem to linger only in purely literary evocations of the painting.[37] In fact, the repudiation of this tradition relies on a basic principle of economy – the existence of Italian models as far more obvious points of reference, models which are clearly all the more significant when they were contemporary with, and hence probably familiar to, El Greco.[38]

It is certainly true that, given the dramatic possibilities suggested by the commission, the expressive reserve El Greco imposed on himself is somewhat unexpected. According to Gómez Moreno, this constraint equates to a return to the realism of a Giotto or a Fra Angelico, towards 'the un-adorned and guileless intimacy that makes the creations of the Middle Ages so pleasing to us'.[39] But the powerful originality of the composition is fundamentally rooted in this regression; comparable in certain respects to treatments of similar themes by contemporaries such as Raphael, Titian or Tintoretto, to mention only those most likely to have influenced El Greco, the painting nevertheless in some way stands apart from all of these.[40]

This expressive reserve, so reminiscent of the early Italian painters, and the striking verticality of the entire composition,

which avoids any reference to the ground and any suggestion of depth, may in fact appear to be the most immediately startling features of the work. Each has the effect of intensify-ing an atmosphere of heightened and mystical spirituality. El Greco's renunciation of emotive effects is certainly remarkable in an artist quite familiar with the spectacular treatments of similar themes by Raphael, Titian and Tintoretto, and it was this restraint which, as mentioned above, so forcefully reminded Gómez Moreno of some early Italian painters. I share Wethey's view that these compositional features belong to the same tradition of medieval revivalism that inspired cer-tain late Mannerist artists, in particular, Zuccaro. Their artistic doctrine was even imbued with quite unmistakably scholastic elements.[41] The publication of El Greco's notes written in the edition Zuccaro gave him of Vasari's *Lives* only confirms this hypothesis.[42] The emotional reserve of the *Burial* may also, however, have a specifically Spanish dimension, as Gómez Moreno suggests in his description of the air of mundane normality with which the supernatural is endowed:

He composed the scene with an apparent normality that seems to include the miracle, arriving at a solution in which the supernatural is made human by contact with the human, and the celestial, in contrast, is freely exalted.[43]

Contemporary parallels are nevertheless hard to find for the remarkable structure somewhat resembling an ogee arch with a triangle formed by the figures of the triumphant Christ flanked by the Virgin and St John the Baptist at its apex. This arch opens out among the clouds like the curtains of a pavilion sheltering the impressive parade of figures below – a rather uncommon structure, particularly in its architec-tonic suggestion of a return to archaic forms. The effect of this regression, which might also be referred to as revival or primitivism, is to form a parallel to the expressive reserve of the figures discussed above.

This latter aspect of the composition being more con-spicuous than the former, I have set out to emphasize the Gothic aspect of what we might call the tectonic structure by describing it as resembling an ogee arch. Variants of this form, including many Toledan examples, abounded in the flamboyant Gothic Spain in which El Greco lived. Not only is this formal connection, to my mind, obvious, but it also accords closely with the elongated and sinuous figurative canon of Michelangelesque Mannerism for which El Greco expresses so much enthusiasm in his notes on Vasari's *Lives*.[44] Both in theory and in practice, Mannerism, as already stated, derived inspiration in many ways from the Gothic, a style that only relatively slowly disappeared in Spain; Spanish spirituality has indeed never lost its primitivist emotional character, and the country has likewise always remained resolutely anti-classical in sensibility.[45]

This reserved but nevertheless profoundly emotional expression also marries with the Gothic-inspired architectonic structure of the composition of the *Burial*. Despite the obvious differences of period and place, the synthesis or harmony between the two aspects of the painting reminds us of the *Madonna della Misericordia* at the centre of the Sansepolcro altarpiece by Piero della Francesca. In this famous work the Virgin stretches out her arms, sheltering within her mantle eight figures kneeling in two symmetrical groups below her. Here we can see the same mixture of contained intensity and strongly individualized, realistic features, and the self-contained absorption of each figure, despite being part of a cohesive group witnessing an event together, is a striking feature of both works.

The Burial of the Count of Orgaz thus takes the irrational aspect of Spanish Mannerism to such an extreme point that, as Wethey reminds us, the ground disappears and there is no suggestion of any kind of perspective depth. But El Greco also breaks even more completely, if that is possible, with the Italian models of Raphael, Titian and Tintoretto in the absence of communication, or perhaps rather in the sublimely perfunctory communication between the figures, each appearing to be alone, self-contained and, as it were, simply juxtaposed.[46]

Cossío, first and foremost of the rediscoverers of El Greco's genius, was ahead of his time in his understanding of this aspect of the work. His description of the painting emphasizes the originality of its composition:

Thirty figures completely fill the scene: those in the background are so compactly grouped together, and those in the foreground are arranged with such art, that not the smallest detail can be seen which might identify the place where the miracle happened. These figures are in fact thirty portraits with no background, an arrange-

ment new at this time and one which incidentally is rarely encountered in the works of this or indeed of any period. The scheme of concentrating attention on the purely human reaches its apogee in this work, to the point that even the little mound of earth under Jesus' feet in the *Espolio (Disrobing of Christ)* has disappeared from the *Burial*. The image has not only been clearly visualized, but furthermore, and fortunately, it has been *considered* and *composed*. This degree of terse simplicity, of naked sincerity and harmonious equilibrium could be achieved only by a long period of gestation in the mind of the artist. While the figures are entirely naturalistic and contemporary, there is in the composition no trace of the classical formulae then in common use, nor of any redundant devices. The student wishing to gain a clear understanding of the extreme contrast between the *Burial* and the painting of its period, and the important innovations it introduced, has only to compare it with any of the great works of the age. Especially apt for the purposes of this analysis would be a work similar in value and subject-matter to the Toledan canvas and which, like Tintoretto's *Miracle of St Mark*, for example, may even have had some influence on El Greco during his training.... Does anything in this work [Cossío refers here to the lower half of the painting] resemble the ceaseless mobility, the violence, indeed the theatricality of Italian painting after Perugino and Bellini? With the works of earlier artists, however, similarities can be found – most notably in its clarity of presentation, calm dignity, symmetrical distribution of volumes, realist sincerity, and a studied monotony. Once artless and unaffected, now more deliberate, these qualities are inseparable from the artist's complete surrender to the all-pervading spontaneity of the natural.[47]

Nearly a hundred years later, despite a whole industry of research dedicated to the *Burial*, the essential features of Cossío's passionate defence of the painting's compositional originality now seem beyond dispute. The experts have confined themselves to the examination of particular influences and connections between specific positions and figures. An example which might be adduced is provided by the group of figures in the foreground formed by St Stephen, St Augustine and the dead Lord of Orgaz, which has been linked to Titian's *Entombment of Christ*.[48] Formal devices, however, have received less attention; the conspicuously Mannerist strategy, for example, whereby the main action of the painting is placed slightly off-centre, has been virtually overlooked. It has the effect of shifting the group in the foreground slightly to the left, forming a steep diagonal that dynamically relates two fundamental compositional elements. These are the rhomboid oval made by the figures of Christ, the Virgin, John the Baptist and the angel bearing the soul of the dead man (a grouping which might be compared to an elongated egg standing on its base) and the foreground oval composed of the saints and the body of Don Gonzalo Ruiz. This latter oval is less elongated because it is at eye level, or is at least nearer to the viewer, and it is inclined slightly to the left.

These elliptical configurations create a quite extraordinary sense of movement within the atmosphere of calm, at times almost hieratical, solemnity which the painting emanates, especially in the lower half. The figures appear to be self-contained, as if set down side by side rather than interacting with one another; similarly, the ovoid shapes give an impression of self-sufficiency, rather than being interconnected by a play of elaborate and vertiginous aerodynamics. It is as if the centrifugal forces with which the zone of celestial glory is unfurled, and the centripetal forces which compress the terrestrial group of figures surrounding the miracle, were autonomous, superimposed upon and separate from the rest of the action. It should also be observed that this earthly semicircle of figures makes a kind of solid barrier around the supernatural event. Densely packed together, although cut off just above the feet, the full-length figures surround or encompass the central event like the drum of a dome.

Does a description of these elements of the painting, however, allow us to appreciate the extraordinary subtlety with which El Greco harmonized the different elements and the two sections of the composition? In this regard, although the equilibrium between the figures in the lower half has rightly been much discussed, in my view insufficient attention has been given to the subtle and exceptionally beautiful counterbalancing of the portrait heads – those incisive, pointed heads so characteristic of El Greco. Some lean slightly to the right, others to the left; imaginary lines projected upwards from them generate a close-knit mesh of intersecting diagonals in the upper part of the picture. This continuous frieze of heads, strangely crowded and almost wedged together, can also be seen as a horizontal line broken at its centre by a vertical crest intersecting an exquisitely subtle arrangement of flame-like curves like the central point of an ogee arch. Now the tightly compressed semicircle of figures surrounding the supernatural event as solidly as the drum of a cupola appears with the effect of a rolling wave, comparable in its volumetric impact to the baroque drum of the dome of S. Ivo della

Sapienza by Francesco Borromini. This architect was another enthusiast of the Gothic, and also a passionate devotee of the ogee arch, of geometrical arrangements involving triangles and circles, of counterposed forces, of Michelangelesque design, and of naturalistic detailing.

The parallel between the compositional structure of the painting of the *Burial* by the eccentric and isolated El Greco and the architecture of the no less eccentric and isolated Borromini in my view goes beyond the kind of incidental formal similarities I have outlined. Without straying too far from our main theme, we might at this point recall my discussion of the architectonic structure of the *Burial*. I likened it to a pavilion with hangings suspended from the top of an arch, a primitivist structure that recalls the precedent of the *Madonna della Misericordia* by Piero della Francesca, where a similar arrangement is found; I could equally well have cited the same artist's *Madonna del Parto* in the cemetery chapel at Monterchi. These images should be compared with the Oratory of S. Filipo Neri by Borromini, and with his account of the conception of its façade, which he describes as like a man with outstretched arms. Commenting on this description, Anthony Blunt emphasized what seemed to him the most remarkable feature of this façade, the fact that it was built on a continuously curving plan.[49] Precisely this arrangement is found in the group of figures in the lower part of the *Burial*, which thus constitutes the base or plan upon which the whole edifice rests.

Still further aspects of compositional structure connect the painter of the *Burial* with Borromini; the delight displayed by both artists in the play of interconnected elements, shapes and figures also embraced the effects of this dialectic. Shifting rhythms generated by the development of the entire composition emerge and unfurl in a dynamic of progressive and vertiginous acceleration. Rising across the picture, these rhythms become increasingly abrupt and disconnected; but complementing the constantly de-centred ascending movement of this vertical modulation is an equally contradictory tension between opposed centripetal and centrifugal forces, between implosion and explosion.

Something of this nature is perhaps suggested by Manuel Gómez Moreno in his perceptive interpretation of the *Burial* as a kind of melodic poem in three movements. His own words are worth quoting here:

The *Burial* could be translated into a kind of symphonic poem in three movements ...: first the funeral procession with its solemn, measured rhythm; singing of offices, prayers. Suddenly the miraculous intervention, silent, as in a dream; we fall into a meditative trance; an appearance of normality keeps both phases in contact. But in the world of the spirits resurrection melodies can be heard; the divine tribunal goes to receive the virtuous soul of the Lord of Orgaz, freed of its earthly garb. Between this and earlier scenes lies the abyss of the supernatural. The dominant tone reaches its greatest intensity and an emotion radiates throughout which can only be expressed in sheer contrast to the terrestrial: light, colours, shapes, although necessarily relying on the material, must be made extreme in order to transport us towards the immaterial. El Greco, thinker and master of an astonishingly virtuoso palette, sensed all the magnificence of this idea, and while the lower section is controlled by a perfect balance, the upper part calls for overwhelming discords arousing the strongest emotions. This he intended and this he did. Instead of caressing melodies he wrested jarring stridencies; no more remains to be said.[50]

In Gómez Moreno's beautiful poetic description of the succession of rhythms in the vertical development of the *Burial*, and the change or rupture in the progression of musical rhythms which regulates the composition, from the solemn measure of the first movement to the celestial discords of the last, it is remarkable that virtually everything is explained by means of the analogy between colour and music, rather than with the more closely linked art of architecture. This is despite the fact that, in architecture, rhythm occurs naturally and does not need metaphors.[51] However, Moreno was following here a line of interpretation suggested by Cossío, based on the fundamental and historically controversial contrast between the two parts of the painting, the lower earthly section and the upper heavenly section.[52] He also clearly analyses the conceptual counterpoise regulating each section, even including the contrasting use and application of colour and the different types of brush used in each area. His conclusions cannot be disputed, especially as El Greco himself said that colour was for him the most fundamental aspect of painting, a highly controversial preference and one much contested before the seventeenth century.[53] It was nevertheless his exotic colour combinations and the coldness of their register that most astonished his contemporaries – the very same qualities that were later so highly valued by the leaders of the first avant-

garde movements who began to re-evaluate his reputation.[54] I must nevertheless emphasize that the 'unity and synthesis' between the two parts of the *Burial* that Cossío and his followers defended so passionately also have an absolutely sound basis in the architectonic structure of the composition. This factor is of particular significance given that, at this point in his career, in the middle of the 1580s, El Greco had yet to advance beyond preoccupations with the volumetric aspects of painting.

In conclusion, the comparison between the cases of El Greco and Borromini is pertinent here not only because of the striking formal similarities between detailed aspects of their works, but also because both artists were notoriously fiery and extravagant characters. Each found himself plunged in a profound crisis that was as much personal as historical, and each responded to this crisis in the same way, with the vigour of original talent, and at the same time from a position of eccentricity and isolation. This, in all probability, was the root cause of the incomprehension that both were to suffer. It is true that Borromini was born more than half a century after El Greco, but they had much ideological common ground. Both were adherents of anti-classicism, Neoplatonism and Counter-Reformation religious sensibility; both admired Mannerist rigour and the drawing of Michelangelo, mixing the archaic with the futuristic, relying equally on imagination and the reinstatement of *praxis*. And finally, Giulio Carlo Argan's analysis of Borromini's conception of perspective applies equally well, in my view, to the composition of *The Burial of the Count of Orgaz*:

Borromini's perspective, although developed in accordance with the most rigorous geometric logic, has the effect of contracting or simply eliminating space.[55]

In sum, although separated by half a century, both artists were isolated and in advance of their time, and both were effectively outsiders.

To recapitulate, then, the unity or synthesis established between the two clearly differentiated parts of the *Burial* corresponds to the dichotomy between the natural and the supernatural. The lower section is horizontal, with the great array of figures befitting the solemn funeral service of an important noble;[56] above, the emphatic verticality of the open heavens is dominated by an isosceles triangle, the figure of Christ enthroned in triumph at its apex. Still further pictorial effects await analysis: for example, the contrast between the shadowy, nocturnal atmosphere of the earthly scene – depicted with an almost complete absence of background detail, which makes it impossible to tell if this is the darkness of an empty night sky or that of a crypt – and the dazzling luminosity above. El Greco is thus able to paint this light with all the startling wonderment at his command. The darkness enveloping the lower section is illuminated more brightly by the brilliant aura emanating from the glowing vestments of the saints and the officiating priest than by the white blaze of the tapers burning in the shadows. Neumeyer has noted that the 'modern' fascination with moonlight, of which this is an instance, was also evinced, contemporaneously, by certain Shakespearean dramas, such as *Hamlet* and *Macbeth*.[57] This predilection was shared by other Mannerist painters in addition to El Greco, such as Luca Cambiaso, as well as by the Carravaggists in their reaction against Mannerism.

The contrast between these two types of illumination also dominates the chromatic tonalities regulating each part of the painting. Thus we can enjoy a conventional Venetian palette – warm, rich, strongly contrasted and even opulent – in some areas of detail on the terrestrial level, while the colours in the heavenly vault are cold and almost watery; this latter aspect perhaps showing the influence of Giulio Clovio, the miniaturist from Croatia who was El Greco's patron in Rome. Thus the experience of contrast between the terrestrial-material region and the celestial-immaterial realm is further heightened.

Given the fundamental importance which, as a true Venetian, El Greco ascribed to colour, these contrasts should be examined a little more closely. The lower section is dominated by exquisite shades in a harmony of black, white and gold, with the 'straw-coloured flesh tones' [*carnaciones pajicientas*] described by Gómez Moreno. There are, in fact, two kinds of black and red; if we look closely at the subtle colours of the embroideries, we can also distinguish a violet, a green and a light blue. In the upper zone the predominant colours are blue, a sulphurous yellow, carmine, various shades of grey and, crowning the whole, the transparent white emanating from the light of Christ. Besides these different registers of colour and tone, yet another important effect is achieved by the refined and magnificent chromaticism that El Greco deploys in the lower part of the painting, where it seems nothing is prohibited and every sensual allurement is permissible; as we look up, this opulence and the virtuosity which gives such pleasure to the senses fade away. Even the handling of the paint reflects this transmutation; the careful finish of the lower zone with its precise, meticulous brushwork disentegrates and breaks up in the loosely painted upper zone, where a careless and vehement spontaneity leaves visible brushstrokes and surface marks.

Gómez Moreno has made a most convincing analysis of El Greco's painterly technique and, although it applies to his work in general, I believe it is worth quoting in full here:

The priming of the canvas is always chestnut brown, in oil, apparently using ochre and umber. Nothing is visible of the drawing, except in his last works when he guided himself simply with traces of umber laid in with the brush to indicate outlines. He sketched in white, red earth, ochre and umber, in mixed neutral tones ranging from reddish dun to brownish grey, which are smeared in separate brushstrokes over the edges of the canvas, doubtless as a way of cleaning the brush. In the flesh tints, the shadows are worked wet in wet with umber and carmine over a medium tint mixing green and pink. The pink and white flesh tones, however, are brushed over almost dry, in accordance with the Byzantine techniques inherited by the medieval Tuscan schools. The clothes were first laid in in white, then their colours applied separately, enriched by many thin layers of paint to become what was called *bañado* [glazed]. The highly prized and expensive ultramarine blue was used over white, perhaps in a mixture with smalt, itself mixed with white for the sky. Carmine is sometimes laid over a brown and pink sketch as a glaze and sometimes used to create a block of solid colour in the shadows, certainly with the addition of litharge (lead monoxide) as a drying agent, because it is well known that on its own it does not dry. The straw-coloured yellow is darkened with ochre. Purple, a mixture of carmine and smalt, is little used. There is even less green, red lead, and pure black: these colours are not found in the *Burial*. The limpid tonality retained by all the colours is admirable, and if overall they have a yellow cast, this is because of a slightly tinted varnish, perhaps used precisely in order to soften the contrasts. For it should be noted that paintings by El Greco which have been cleaned too thoroughly, such as the one at Illescas, are unpleasantly crude and cold.[58]

Moving on now from contrasts in colour, we can still find many other ways in which the two parts of the painting are counterpointed, for example in the contrast between the profound and unprecedented realism of the figures attending the funeral and the fluid, attenuated features of the stylized celestial beings. This realism has earned the superb group of likenesses its place as one of the most direct precursors, both in form and in content, of what has come to be seen as the naturalistic prototype of the Spanish portrait.[59] A further contrast is to be seen between the hieratic, measured and solemn atmosphere of the compact lower group around the dead knight and the saints holding him and the strident, spiralling radiance of the figures strewn disharmoniously among the clouds in the upper part.

The extreme contrast or dissonance between the two parts of the painting later led to the decline in critical esteem which the *Burial* quite unjustly suffered until its 'rediscovery' at the beginning of this century, as we shall see in due course. Even writers almost contemporary with El Greco considered the work a product of the utmost extravagance. In time there would be accusations of madness, clumsy mishandling and incompetence. Those who voiced these criticisms not only failed to appreciate the extraordinary difficulty of painting this subject in the restricted space allowed, but above all were blind to the conceptual and compositional originality which El Greco brought to his resolution of the exacting demands laid down in the commission.

It is certainly quite natural that any viewer of the painting should immediately be drawn to the superb gallery of portraits in the funeral party. At eye level, the row of faces is beautifully set off against the black line of their doublets, and all seem to be illuminated by the golden glow emanating from the magnificent vestments worn by St Augustine and St Stephen in their liturgical functions as, respectively, bishop and deacon. Taking the lifeless body of the Lord of Orgaz in their arms, they support him effortlessly, despite the fact that he wears a complete set of shining damascened armour, a detail which naturally attracted attention because it also contrasts with the ponderous weight usually imparted to such scenes at this period.[60]

The spectator's eyes genuinely light up with the glorious richness of this foreground trio and with the amazing naturalism of the faces of the figures surrounding it. The three central figures form a symmetrical oval and the figures of the two saints are held in a beautifully measured balancing move-

ment; at its centre, the foreshortened and equally impressive figure of the dead nobleman is suspended. His outline completes the curve; from the space at its very centre an exquisitely beautiful hand emerges from a cuff of the finest lace with all the delicate expressivity of a black-and-white cameo. The vivid flesh tones of this hand contrast with the grey pallor of the corpse's face; the noble and clearly delineated features are imbued with the serene beatitude of the dead.

The beauty of this trio has powerfully drawn the attention of all who have seen it, and the great delight El Greco took in painting the vestments has been generally observed. He seems to luxuriate in the fine details and lavish colouring, combining, in the Venetian tradition, the purest refinement with a rich sensuality. This opulence gradually fades away and finally disappears from the rest of the painting. The saints do not have haloes and their liturgical robes of yellow and white brocade are of the period. St Stephen's dalmatica, wonderfully embroidered with golden threads over crimson, is embellished with a scene attached to the lower part of his robe that forms a miniature painting in its own right. It represents the saint's own martyrdom; he is shown on his knees being stoned by hired killers, who are naked, as is Saul, seated on the left, while the image of the Holy Trinity appears above. St Augustine's episcopal cope has the same fine embroidery and bears the images of Saints Peter, James and Catherine. How, lastly, can one describe the shining damascened armour of the Lord of Orgaz and its beautiful reflections, except to say that here the painter clearly did not wish to stint any form of sensual delight. This group, with all its glittering gold, effectively forms a self-contained incident within the painting.

Moving on from the superabundantly attractive brilliance of the protagonists of the miracle, the viewer will not be disappointed on turning to the frieze of heads of the figures surrounding it. The meticulous and harmoniously composed alignment is broken only by the two large full-length figures standing a little forward of the extraordinary event. On the left is a meditative Franciscan friar, seen in profile in his grey habit; on the right is the priest who is officiating at the ceremony in the role of an auxiliary, as denoted by his transparent surplice. Opening his arms in wonder, with his back almost to the viewer, he looks up in astonishment at the sky – the only one of the thirty or so people represented here to do so openly. Also out of alignment is the small figure of a boy on the left, standing out in front in a low foreground plane that advances towards the viewer; he holds a burning taper in a typically Mannerist twist of his right hand. With his left hand he points to the supernatural event, presenting it to us, and thus acting as a respectful attendant whose role is to introduce the drama – another conventional device characteristic of Mannerism.

All in all, it might be thought that the compact, continuous frieze of notables with their faces so closely crowded together would induce an effect of monotony, were it not, as I have already emphasized, one of the most astoundingly realist collections of portrait heads ever painted; a collection of faces, moreover, which depicts as few have done what might be called the Spanish human prototype of the period. In fact, the absolute verism with which each face is portrayed is such that the curiosity the painting later kindled about the identity of the figures is immediately comprehensible, because, even without any previous knowledge of the work, no one could doubt that all the figures depicted in it are real Toledan personalities of the period.

The figures in the painting

ALTHOUGH THERE HAS been much speculation on this matter, to this day only two or three of the portrait figures can be identified with any certainty. Firstly, the kneeling boy in the left foreground is assumed to be El Greco's son, Jorge Manuel, because of the folded handkerchief protruding from his pocket which bears the painter's signature in Greek – *doménikos theotokópolis epoíei*: 'Domenikos Theotokopoulos made this' – followed by the date 1578, the year of the boy's birth. Also firmly identified is the profile of the man with a grey beard on the opposite side of the painting, above the left shoulder of the auxiliary priest in the transparent white surplice. This figure can be recognized from other portraits of him by El Greco as Antonio de Covarrubias, a humanist priest and a friend of the artist.[61]

Leaving aside for the moment the question of the truth or otherwise of the various proposed identifications of the other figures, which I shall go on to discuss later, their attire and in some cases their bearing leave no doubt as to their class, rank and office. Thus we can state that the funeral cortège consists of priests, nobles and men of letters. The former include lay clergy, celebrants in the ceremony, and monks – a Franciscan, an Augustinian and a Dominican. Three of the nobles are readily identified as such by the red crosses of the Order of Santiago embroidered on their black doublets. Two at least of the intellectuals are recognizable by their high collars, one being Antonio de Covarrubias, whom we have already discussed, while the older and more worn features of the face visible between the black-cowled Augustinian and the beardless Dominican on the other side of the painting appear to be those of his brother, Diego de Covarrubias, who died in 1577.[62] Some writers, however, including Gómez Moreno, have argued that this figure is the parish priest of Santo Tomé, Andrés Núñez of Madrid, a claim which seems most implausible.[63]

To embark, then, on the task of identifying the various remaining figures – an endeavour which in most cases, as I have emphasized, is based merely on conjecture – starting at our left, we come first to the head of a stout man standing behind the hooded Franciscan: he is thought to be Juan López de la Quadra, then master of the building works at the church of Santo Tomé. To the right of the Dominican monk (one of the few in this group who is shown looking upwards, in a way which suggests the rapt absorption of the mystic) appears a face which, it has been argued, might be El Greco's self-portrait. The same claim has been made for the next figure, standing immediately behind the main action of the painting. Distinguished by the open gesture of his delicately poised hands, as well as by the ostentatiously displayed cross of Santiago, he has been tentatively accorded the title of mayor of Toledo, since he is without doubt the most important of the local notables of the day depicted here.

Of the group of nobles and gentlemen crowded together at the centre of the picture, the six in the foreground are all comparatively young, some in the prime of life, one hardly more than a boy;[64] all wear black doublets with starched ruffs, pleated or embellished with fine lace, and all have the same expression of elegant hauteur, sometimes pallid, exalted and almost fanatical, while others are serenely imperturbable and somewhat distant. At all events, this formidable gallery of portraits, as has often been stated, is arguably one of the earliest and finest representations of the formal and psychological prototype of Spanish *hidalguía* (nobility).

Let us turn now to the right-hand side of the picture where, between the figure already identified as Antonio de Covarrubias and the priest in the transparent surplice, there is a face with upturned eyes that is thought to be a portrait of the scholar Francisco de Pisa, whose colourful writings about the miracle of the Lord of Orgaz, the church of Santo Tomé and the *Burial* itself have been quoted earlier.[65] A figure we have referred to more than once is that of the auxiliary priest, with back turned and arms outstretched, who, as Cossío points out, is identified as Pedro Ruiz Durón in the long inscription at the foot of the canvas.[66] Finally, at the extreme right, the principal officiant in the ceremony is designated as such by his cope embroidered in gold over black, as befits the funeral liturgy, and with medallions on its border showing in one the skull and crossbones of Calvary, and in another St Thomas holding a carpenter's square. We see this figure in profile, his eyes lowered to read from the book held open before him. Given these details, we can have no hesitation in identifying this cleric as Don Andrés Núñez of Madrid, priest of Santo Tomé, zealous litigant on behalf of the parish, and the man responsible for commissioning the painting.

We might go on to add still more suggestions and hypotheses proposing putative identifications of the portraits. Among these are Astrana Marín's attractive but totally unfounded claim that one of the participants might be no less a figure than Miguel de Cervantes,[67] a claim based on the fact that the writer was living in Toledo at the time when the picture was painted. Another more modest attribution, based on equally flimsy evidence, seeks to show that Manusso, El Greco's brother, appears in the painting; however, this is chronologically impossible, since he did not arrive in Toledo until 1591. None of these speculations adds to our understanding of the work, nor are they even remotely credible; it would therefore be unproductive to spend any more time on the subject.

We find ourselves on iconographically surer ground when we look to the upper section of the picture, depicting the heavenly Glory, to identify the supernatural beings enthroned there. The first figure we encounter, rising with spread wings through a narrow gap between the clouds, displays a foreshortened torsion reminiscent of the exalted Mannerism of Tintoretto. Immediately recognizable as an angel, this figure is conspicuous by its dramatic central position in the composition, forming part of an oblique vertical movement linking the inert body of the Lord of Orgaz with the figure of Christ. This angel bears in its arms the soul of the dead man, represented as a kind of transparent chrysalis in the shape of a newborn baby, the guise then thought to correspond most closely to those beings who enjoyed the privilege of going directly to heaven.[68]

We have described elsewhere the principal group consisting of the three largest figures who form a triangle at the pinnacle of the Glory. This grouping of Christ, the Virgin Mary and St John the Baptist traditionally appears in scenes of the Last Judgment. On the right, immediately behind St John the Baptist, we recognize St Paul, wearing a pinkish-orange cloak over a blue-violet tunic. As a pendant to the latter, we see opposite him the unmistakable figure of St Peter in a striking yellow cloak with the famous keys hanging from his right hand. He is set slightly higher than St Paul, both saints being supported by the same oblique cloud formation which diagonally intersects this part of the Glory.

A wonderful cold light pervading the whole heavenly choir emanates from the dazzling whiteness of the resurrected Christ, enthroned in a shining white shroud above the central axis of the composition. The span of His outstretched arms seems to embrace the two principal figures of the merciful Last Judgment, and also draws together – in a series of ever-widening imaginary lines – the remaining personages of greatest importance in the hierarchy, including Saints Peter and Paul. The most diverse range of figures can be recognized in other celestial episodes, although depicted in varying positions and on different scales, some higher, some lower, some central, some off-centre. Among the multitude crowded in dense rows behind St Paul we first detect St Thomas with his huge carpenter's square, garbed in a greenish tunic with a pale-yellow cloak. His prominence is obviously justified by his being the titular saint of the church. The fourth figure from the right in the same row is none other than Philip II, whose presence here has been mistakenly interpreted as an indication of the painter's generosity or lack of resentment, despite having been so recently spurned by the monarch. Some writers, such as Hugo Kehrer, have tried to make out portraits of Pope Sixtus V and the archbishop of Toledo himself, Gaspar de Quiroga,[69] in the crowded multitude of faces in the distance, while Gómez Moreno also detects Juan Pardo Tavera, an earlier incumbent of the archbishopric.[70] A trio of indistinct figures set below and to the right of this throng consists of a naked man with two women, one of whom is immediately recognizable as Mary Magdalen with her crystal jar of scented ointment. The identity of the second woman is less obvious, although she may well be Mary's companion Martha. The contorted posture of the naked male figure suggests that he could be either St Sebastian or the resurrected Lazarus, a figure more relevant to the theme of the painting.

To round off this description of the heavenly beings, three figures among the host of anonymous angels, shown in every conceivable position, remain to be examined. Supported by a cloud at the extreme left, below and behind St Peter and the Virgin Mary, they are identified by their attributes as David, Moses and Noah: one plays the harp, the second holds aloft the tablets of the law, and the third places his right hand on the ark.

From the iconographical point of view, this programme generally conforms fairly closely with the traditional vision of heaven on the Day of Judgment. In compositional terms, however, many writers have attempted to interpret this Glory as a direct derivation from Byzantine models, and specifically from the Mistra *Dormition of the Virgin*, dated around 1360.[71] But, as Wethey has conclusively argued, this interpretation is demonstrably fallacious. The contemporary Italian provenance of most of the elements deployed by El Greco in *The Burial of the Count of Orgaz* is, after all, immediately recognizable. This does not, however, detract in the least from the work's powerful originality, manifest in the artist's success in creating something uniquely his own from models today classified as Mannerist.[72]

Critical fortune

ONE THING, at all events, is quite clear: the critical trend today that perceives an Eastern influence as dominating El Greco's mature work is a mirror image of the impulse to exoticize that was also endemic in past criticism – with the difference that what was once deprecated is now a source of positive admiration. In fact, the most powerful determining factor for this school of thought has not been El Greco's colourful life, his reputation as an extravagant personality or his highly personal painterly manner, but almost three centuries of negative criticism, during which, as often occurs in such cases, legend has prospered at the expense of reality. For this reason, the analysis and understanding of the critical fortune of *The Burial of the Count of Orgaz* are as revealing as they are essential.

As regards the critical fortune of El Greco's work in general, rather than simply that of the Santo Tomé painting, before the modern period (and it has received more attention in the twentieth than in the nineteenth century), very little was written about it, and about three-quarters of this was wholly negative. It is true that El Greco enjoyed a certain local fame during his lifetime, but even this declined during the later years of his Spanish period. The implication is that his star began to wane from around the beginning of the 1590s onwards, as much because of the growing bewilderment that greeted the emergence of his radical late style as because of new directions taken by Spanish artistic taste. A period when he retained a degree of respectful consideration nevertheless lasted at least until the beginning of the seventeenth century, as is shown by descriptions of his work by local writers such as Francisco de Pisa and a number of his friends, among them some of the greatest literary talents such as Luis de Góngora and Hortensio Félix de Paravicino. We also have the account by Francisco Pacheco, whose praise is somewhat qualified (see below).

Nevertheless, on reading the comments of Fray José de Sigüenza on El Greco, the reservations implicit in some earlier accolades – the precise words of the lawyer Juan de Butrón, for example, are: 'Dominico Greco, whose works in some opinions at least deserve praise'[73] – and, above all, the unaccountable silence about the painter in such treatises as that by Vicente Carducho, whose *Diálogos de la Pintura*, published in 1633, a mere nineteen years after El Greco's death, makes no mention of him,[74] we can only conclude that, in all truth, he had never really been fully understood.

In fact, of those who knew El Greco personally when he was approaching old age, the writer who appears to have taken him most seriously was Francisco Pacheco, who was himself also a painter. He refers to El Greco at various points in his *Arte de la Pintura*, and also wrote an encomium in his memory, now sadly lost.[75] At all events, the reservations he voices over El Greco's disagreeable manner and his preference for colour over drawing, as well as many other opinions which seemed to him equally extravagant, and above all the preference he records for his paintings made 'on smaller canvases', indicate the situation sufficiently clearly to prepare us for the painter's subsequent disrepute.[76]

It comes then as no surprise that, in the opinion of Jusepe Martínez, whose *Discursos practicables del nobilísimo arte de la pintura* were written around 1673, El Greco was essentially an *extravagante*, whose works were so strange and so wilful that they created confusion even among initiates, and so dissimilar from each other that 'they do not seem to be by the same hand'.[77] 'Disagreeable', 'bold' and 'of a harsh nature' were the epithets used by José García Hidalgo towards the end of the century in 1693.[78] Antonio Palomino, the Spanish Vasari, took the same view and illustrated this developing critical tradition with copious anecdotes and examples. He nevertheless wrote a long biographical study of El Greco, in which the information given and opinions expressed have influenced most later writing about the artist up to the present day.[79]

It is notable, moreover, that Pacheco, Martínez, García Hidalgo and Palomino were all painters – particularly significant as an indication of the 'fatal critical disdain' endured by El Greco, to use Mancini's phrase. However this may be, a reference by Palomino to *The Burial of the Count of Orgaz* is of especial interest not only because he praises the part containing the portraits, but also for his suggestion that the remaining parts of this and other paintings, dismissed by general accord as 'extravagance', were produced by El Greco in an attempt to distinguish himself from his master, Titian.[80]

From the time of the publication in 1724 of the second part of Palomino's treatise containing the biographies of Spanish artists, there would be no fundamental changes of opinion in the increasingly scarce literature devoted to El Greco until recent times. I refer naturally to critics writing in Spain because, throughout this period, the artist remained completely unknown outside his adopted country. It is true that certain worthy scholars of the Enlightenment, such as Ceán Bermúdez and Llaguno, made a number of interesting points challenging traditional opinions in certain respects, although without concealing their dislike.[81] But, as I suggested earlier, a real critical rediscovery of El Greco did not get under way until the last third of the nineteenth century, gathering pace in the first thirty years of the twentieth. Even the writings championing his cause published during the first two-thirds of the last century by European Romantics as part of what has since become familiar as an exalted Romantic image of Spain relate only tangentially to El Greco, generally in terms of an ill-defined enthusiasm for the same vital, high-spirited extravagance which previously attracted such widespread disdain.[82]

As regards *The Burial of the Count of Orgaz* itself, reiterations of seventeenth-century critical opinions will be found to recur in ever greater length and prolixity. It was considered the major work in El Greco's Spanish period, but this view was based on the extraordinary quality of the portraits in the lower part of the painting, while the upper zone continued to excite condemnation and incomprehension at least until the last decades of the nineteenth century.[83] Finally, thanks both to positivist scientific movements and to the renewal of vision fomented by naturalism and the Impressionists, the traditional view of El Greco, and hence inevitably of the *Burial*, underwent a fundamental change. Certainly crucial to this development was the influence of painters and writers (some of the international stature of Manet, Degas and Cézanne), complemented by a spirit of renovation among critics and art historians which gained pace at the turn of the century.[84]

In Spain, much the same happened as elsewhere: it was the initiatives of *fin-de-siècle* artists such as Ignacio Zuloaga and Santiago Rusiñol,[85] of realist and naturalist writers of the

Restoration such as Benito Pérez Galdós and Emilia Pardo Bazán,[86] as well as most of the movement known as the Generation of 98,[87] that fostered a new approach to El Greco. The critical contribution of their predecessors in the century now drawing to a close, often motivated by a modish Romantic attraction towards the foreign, was not substantial. Notwithstanding this, a truly crucial role was played by the new historiography of the Institución Libre de Enseñanza (Independent Institute of Education) in the critical rehabilitation of El Greco then under way in Spain.[88] It is thus not surprising that the first major book to be published about the painter was written by Manuel Bartolomé Cossío. First published in 1908, it has remained required reading to this day.

Cossío's monograph is a quite extraordinary work from every point of view, as also is the study published by the renowned French writer Maurice Barrès, although his *Greco ou le secret de Tolède* is a more literary evocation. Both books enjoyed huge success and put an end once and for all to the unfavourable critical reception granted to El Greco for so long; they also gave him his present status as one of the greatest geniuses of Western art. It cannot be denied, however, that earlier avant-garde movements, more or less from the first Expressionists onwards, also played a fundamental role, not simply in communicating the value of his work to a general public, but also in facilitating a wider understanding of El Greco and thus overcoming the bewilderment generally felt by non-specialists faced by his distinctive style.[89] In 1881, Federico de Madrazo, then Director of the Prado, described El Greco's paintings as 'horrible caricatures',[90] but from the 1920s onwards his reputation as one of the major artists in Spain's principal museum of art has continued to grow.

The Burial of the Count of Orgaz was the fundamental touchstone within the formidable critical movement that rehabilitated El Greco's artistic reputation; each in its own way, the ground-breaking publications of Cossío and Barrès highlighted the centrality of this work and explicitly vindicated it in its entirety, without disparaging any part of it. Cossío's descriptions in praise of the Glory in the upper part promoted a fuller critical understanding of the *Burial*, but were also important in providing the basis of an approach to the artist's hitherto especially rebarbative late period.[91] In fact, thanks to the renewed attention given to the famously reviled upper section of the painting, El Greco came to be seen not merely as the precursor of Velázquez and of the great tradition of naturalism in Spanish painting, but as the creator of a unique, absolute and universal art. It is true that, even at this time, his 'extravagance' was still often met with a kind of amazement, although now of an admiring kind, and now began to be attributed to defective eyesight or to other physical or even psychological aberrations.[92] Neither these diagnoses, however, nor the more or less novelistic interpretations that, even today, continue to search for esoteric elements in the artist's life or work can impair the general public's understanding and enjoyment of El Greco's paintings.

More recent events concerning the artist naturally include the publication in 1962 of H.E. Wethey's monumental study *El Greco and his School*. Also of great importance were the discovery, documentation and critical editions of El Greco's marginal annotations to two major texts of artistic theory, Vasari's *Lives* and Vitruvius's *De Architectura*, in the Venetian edition by Daniele Barbaro; these commentaries have provided crucial insights into El Greco's thinking on art. We should also highlight the exhibition mounted in the spring of 1982 in Madrid and Toledo, Ohio, with the double title of 'El Greco of Toledo' and 'The Toledo of El Greco'.

As regards the state of conservation of *The Burial of the Count of Orgaz*, the work was protected from theft and other destructive acts for many years, essentially by the painter's longstanding disrepute, and is still in fairly good condition, having been left in its original setting and spared serious abuse. Cossío documents an attempt at restoration in 1672 led by Simón Vicente, consisting in 'having cleaned the painting and renewed the epitaph'.[93] Cossío himself observed that in the middle of the nineteenth century the picture was badly neglected and 'hung with no support from below', but shortly after this was noted it was restored under the direction of Madrazo and Moreno. This restoration apparently took the form of a skilful and most successful new lining of the canvas. In 1943, Gómez Moreno pointed out that 'the limpid tonality retained by all the colours is admirable, and if overall they have a yellow cast, this is because of a slightly tinted varnish, perhaps used precisely in order to soften the contrasts'.[94] At all events, the testimonies of successive generations of visitors rarely mention the painting being in poor condition, although criticisms were made of the setting and the lighting in the chapel and of the general condition of the church of

Santo Tomé. These faults were attended to in time and fortunately the situation today is quite different.

I should mention in conclusion a smaller 'copy' or 'replica' of the *Burial* which has been in the Prado since 1902, after more than a hundred years in the Academia de San Fernando. It was taken there in 1774 after the confiscation of goods following the expulsion of the Jesuits. Palomino observes that:

in the Jesuit house in the same city there is another painting also by his hand and of the same theme, but without the Glory above,

which was made by Dominico in response to requests from those fathers as a token of their gratitude for the donation of land for their church by the Count of Orgaz ... and in truth both pictures look as if they were by Titian.[95]

However, the work now in the Prado does not even remotely resemble a work by El Greco, even less one by Titian, as has in fact been noted in catalogues of the collection since 1920, where it is recorded as a 'copy by his son Jorge Manuel'.[96] This work, significantly enough, is not signed.

A brief biography

VIRTUALLY UNMENTIONED IN Italian art-historical literature, with the exception of Giulio Mancini's observations, in the second part of his *Considerationi*, that he 'died very old' and '*quasi che svanito nell'arte*' [as if consumed by art], the biography of El Greco is full of gaps and misleading banalities; little substantial information is provided even by contemporary Spanish treatises on art. This situation was only partially remedied during the early years of the twentieth century when El Greco's life and work began to generate widespread interest, leading legions of specialist researchers to explore archives wherever it was thought he might have lived or had some connection.

Despite this formidable international investigative effort, irrefutable facts are few and far between and, apart from the recently discovered autograph notes on the treatises on art and architecture by Vasari and Vitruvius, they mainly relate to legal and financial documents. Thus, the body of available information has remained fragmentary, and is in fact still largely based on Spanish transcriptions made at the beginning of the twentieth century by Cossío, San Román and Zarco Cuevas. This lack of direct information has ultimately led to too great a reliance on inference and supposition in piecing together a story of the life of El Greco.

It is reasonable to assume, at all events, that Domenikos Theotokopoulos – the alternative forms used by the painter to sign his name were 'Theotokopolis', 'Theotoskopoli' or 'Theotokopoli' – was born in 1541, or at the end of 1540, in Candia, capital of the island of Crete, then under Venetian rule. His father, a certain Jorghi, died in 1556. We also know that he had a brother called Manusso, who came to Spain in 1591 and settled in Toledo for good; he died there in 1604, having stayed away from his homeland because of pressures of debt. This fact, together with what we know about his position as a tax-collector for the Republic of Venice, allows us to describe El Greco's family milieu as one of middle-class government employees.

The next important phase of El Greco's life begins with his arrival in Venice, probably during the 1560s, although the exact date of his journey, as well as what he actually did there, is very unclear. It is by no means certain that a letter from Titian to Philip II referring to a brilliant 'disciple' of the Italian artist relates to our painter. In fact, the only definitive document dating from that time and still extant is a lawyer's certificate situating El Greco in Candia on 6 June 1566, which also informs us that he had already earned the title of '*maestro*'. Equally problematic is a supposed reference to him in a letter from his patron, the Croatian miniaturist Giulio Clovio, purportedly recommending him in Rome. However, documentary evidence does exist to show that El Greco was living in that city in 1572; he is listed in the register of the local Accademia di San Luca. Between this date and 1577, when his presence in Spain is well established, we can only speculate; even the motives ascribed to his journey to Spain are conjectural. It may well have been suggested by a Spanish priest and canon of the cathedral of Toledo, Pedro Chacón, or by a friend of the latter, Luis de Castilla; equally, the move may have been motivated by the hope of obtaining commissions at the monastery of the Escorial, like several of his Italian colleagues.

Given this paucity of solid information, the details supplied by Mancini's account are particularly important; he tells us that El Greco was in Rome during the pontificate of Pius V, having come there from Venice, where he had made a particular study of 'the things of Titian'. He also recounts that his early days in the city were artistically promising, but that on one occasion, in the course of a discussion about covering over some of the nudes in Michelangelo's *Last Judgment*, El Greco dared to say, in public, that if this work were to be destroyed he would be capable of replacing it '*con honestà et decenza non inferiore a quella di bontà di pintura*' [with honesty and decency, and making as good a painting]. According to Mancini's testimony, the furious reaction this provoked among local painters obliged El Greco to leave for Spain.

The first documents locating the artist in Spain date from 1577; first in Madrid and then, almost immediately afterwards, in Toledo. He settled there and remained until his death on 7 April 1614. During the thirty-seven years of his residence in Spain El Greco did not travel anywhere, apart from short trips within the province, the furthest being to Madrid or at most, possibly, to Seville. Apart from the fact of his residence in Spain, we know little about his friendships, way of life or other personal details, except that he formed an amorous liaison with Jerónima de las Cuevas, who came from a well-off family, and that they had a son, Jorge Manuel, born in 1578. There is no evidence to show that the couple married. He had two pupils in addition, of course, to his son; these were Francisco Preboste and Luis Tristán. The latter had already reached the peak of his abilities and was the only one of the three with any real talent. As mentioned above, El Greco welcomed his brother Manusso in 1591 and kept him at his side until he died. We also know that he frequented the congenial intellectual circles of Toledo, where the poetic eulogies dedicated to him by Góngora and Paravicino reveal that he must have been held in high esteem. Another token of his repute is the visit paid to him by the Sevillian Francisco Pacheco, who wrote one of the few direct descriptions of El Greco, recounting his observations on the mentality, character and artistic opinions of the artist. Finally, he must have been a prodigal spender, if some contemporary accounts, such as that of J. Martínez, describing his epicurean delight in luxury, are to be believed. Certainly this reputation is supported by evidence of the huge income he gained from his work, notwithstanding which he was invariably up to his neck in debt. Most conclusively of all, the inventory of goods made after his death came to a fairly insignificant amount, in terms of material possessions at least.

Most of the remaining documents relating to El Greco concern contracts for commissions, disputes and lawsuits concerning valuations and payment, all kinds of legal declarations, proxy petitions, statements by witnesses in cases not always involving artistic matters, testamentary writs, wills, orders for payment, acknowledgments of debts, rents and leases, purchases of goods, and so on. All these provide us with a framework of documented events of extraordinary value, not only in enabling us to trace a story of the artist's life and his evolving situation, but above all in providing the basis of an enhanced understanding and a more accurate dating of his works. In addition, this evidence allows us to infer many other undocumented developments, such as the waning of his artistic reputation during the last period of his life, around the turn of the century.

El Greco's biography can thus be seen as consisting of six phases, five of which are of particular artistic significance. The first spans the period from 1541 until the middle of the 1560s and includes his infancy and part of his youth; his first artistic steps were taken in his native Crete during this period, although only one or two paintings dating from this time are known. The second phase starts at the end of the 1560s, when he was living in Venice and must have adapted an oriental style of painting in order to conform to the artistic canons of Venetian Mannerism, as a follower of Titian and Tintoretto; few paintings remain from this period and these are still quite crude. During the third phase, from the early 1570s onwards, he was mainly resident in Rome, where he already enjoyed a certain artistic renown; a number of works are known from this period, including some excellent portraits and paintings on religious themes which offer an occasional glimpse of the painter's potential genius, such as *Christ Cleansing the Temple* (1570–72), now in the National Gallery, Washington. The fourth phase, between 1577 and the beginning of the 1580s, saw his move to Spain, initially motivated by the highest ambitions for a role in the court of

Philip II, or at least for important royal commissions at the Escorial; but after the fiasco of *St Maurice*, he turned to a local Toledan clientele and concentrated on meeting their tastes. He was splendidly received in this city, as the extremely important commissions he obtained for the cathedral and the church of Santo Domingo el Antiguo attest. He continued to work primarily as a portraitist during this period, when the clarity and quality of the development of his mature style begin to be seen. In the fifth phase, between 1585 and 1595, he continued to receive important local commissions, in particular *The Burial of the Count of Orgaz*, and his position, from the point of view both of reputation and of income, appears well established. Finally, in the sixth phase, between 1595 and 1614, we witness, on the one hand, the Mannerist radicalization of his painterly style and, on the other, a change of taste on the part of his patrons, together with an increasing physical debility – and, according to some sources, a parallel psychological deterioration. These factors explain El Greco's final decline. He nevertheless went on to create some of his most personal masterpieces, although these were already condemned by some of his contemporaries as 'extravagant'. For several hundred years, almost until our own era, these late works continued to be disparaged and considered the products of madness or sickness, or at best as the works of a painter who attempted to hide a lack of talent and technique beneath a cloak of outlandish artifice.

Notes

1 In fact, with the exception of occasional isolated journeys within the province, and perhaps at the most one or two visits to Madrid, El Greco's residence in Toledo was uninterrupted until his death in 1614, since his supposed stay in Seville seems to be based on mere conjecture and is unsupported by documentary evidence. Thus, even if we accept that he may not have settled in the imperial city until the early 1680s, he nevertheless must have spent more than thirty years there, almost half of his life. At all events, it was in Toledo that he lived for the greatest number of years. The question of stylistic development is naturally more complex, especially because it is obvious that an evolution clearly occurred around the 1590s that enabled El Greco to intensify the anti-realistic elements characteristic of his late style. It was this change that completely disconcerted his contemporaries and subsequently led to his prolonged critical disrepute. Even by the early years of the twentieth century, when no one dared any longer to deny his incontestable genius, this anti-realistic aspect was seen from a medical or psychiatric perspective as stemming from a visual defect or from the onset of paranoia. Nonetheless, all the specialists, from Cossío onwards, coincide in referring to *The Burial of the Count of Orgaz* as a kind of keystone that brings together and explicates the mature development of El Greco's style. While the lower section of the painting consummately and thoughtfully unites the style known as reformed Mannerism with emergent Spanish naturalism, the upper part, showing the heavens, appears to herald the intensification of the anti-realistic element of the painter's final manner. Significantly, it was this aspect of the work which startled everyone who saw it, and which gave rise to interpretations of this late style as deranged. In this sense, the *Burial* is truly a key work in El Greco's development and perhaps that which most closely unites the work of his first period in Spain, that is, of the immediate past, with the exalted artistic future which still lay ahead.

2 Although it is generally thought that El Greco arrived in Venice around 1560, no evidence has been found to support this date; in fact, the only relevant document, published in 1961 by Mertzios, proves the presence of the painter in Candia on 6 June 1566. This implies, among other things, that he could not have been in Venice before 1567. Furthermore, evidence of a connection with Titian is too slight to support the relationship which has been suggested, based on a letter from Titian to Philip II, stating that he hoped soon to complete a commission on which he and his son were working 'together with another very worthy young disciple of mine' (cf. *Tiziano e la Corte di Spagna nei documenti dell'Archivio Generale di Simancas*, Madrid, 1975, p. 101). The evidence provided by the admittedly more explicit letter, dated 19 November 1570, from the Croatian miniaturist Giulio Clovio to Cardinal Alessandro Farnese is also inconclusive. It has been assumed that El Greco is referred to in this letter, which describes 'a young man from Candia, a disciple of Titian' (Sackcinski). However this may be, further Italian references to a connection between El Greco and Titian, as well as the prominence given to it in accounts of his life and work by Spanish writers, suggest that some kind of link must actually have existed. It is likely, however, that this relationship was quite tangential and informal, such as might result from the regular presence of a young admirer in the master's workshop for a year or two. This conclusion is evidently based on the formal indebtedness of El Greco's Italian work to the style of Titian, a dependence which cannot be described as excessive. El Greco certainly did borrow from aTitian, but probably not as much as from Tintoretto.

3 See Giulio Mancini, *Considerazioni sulla pittura* (critical edition by A. Maruchi), Rome, 1956,

vol. 1, pp. 230f. As well as mentioning El Greco's early success in Rome and describing him as 'having studied in Venice and in particular the things of Titian', the writer relates the story of his disgrace following his public disparagement of the artistic value of Michelangelo's *Last Judgment*. According to Mancini, it was this indiscretion that obliged El Greco to leave for Spain.

4   Nineteenth-century writers before Cossío had summarized or transcribed the text of the inscription in their accounts of the *Burial*. Nevertheless, Cossío (in the third note of chapter VII of his book) was the first to copy out the Latin text and follow it with a translation. See M.B. Cossío, *El Greco* (1908), p. 259; subsequent references are to the 1981 Madrid edition.

5   I refer to the famous decree promulgated during the 25th and final session of the Council of Trent, which took place on 3 and 4 December 1564 and dealt 'with the invocation, veneration and relics of the saints and of holy images'. One of the Council's proclamations specifically on this topic was the following: '*Quod ut fidelius observetur, statuit sancta Synodus, nemini licere ullo in loco, vel Ecclesia etiam quomodolibet exempto, ullam insolitam ponere, vel ponemdam curare imaginem, nisi ab Episcopo approbata fuerit*' [That these things may be more faithfully observed, the Holy Council decrees that no one may place, or cause to be placed, any uncommon image anywhere or in any church, howsoever exempt, unless it has been authorized by the bishop](*Acts of the Council of Trent*, XXV, Surius, IV, p. 983).

6   See Fray Jerónimo Román, *Chrónica de la orden de los ermitaños del Glorioso padre Sancto Agustin. Dividida en doze Centurias*, Salamanca, 1569, century 10, year 1327, p. 64.

7   See Francisco de Pisa, *Apuntamientos para la segunda parte de la 'Descripción de la Imperial Ciudad de Toledo'* (based on the manuscript copy by Francisco de Santiago Palomares, with original notes in the hand of Cardinal Lorenzana), edited by José Gómez-Menor, Toledo, 1976, p. 68.

8   See Alonso de Villegas, *Flos Sanctorum. Tercera parte. Historia general en que se escriven las vidas de sanctos extravagantes y de varones Illustres en virtud ...*, Toledo, 1588.

9   See Pedro Alcocer, *Hystoria, o Descripcion de Imperial cibdad de Toledo*, Toledo, 1554, bk II, ch. 21.

10   Cossío, *op. cit.*, p. 110.

11   *Ibid.* p. 112.

12   See Francisco de Borja San Román, *El Greco en Toleda o nuevas investigaciones acerca de la vida y obras de Dominico Theotocopuli*, Madrid, 1910, pp. 142f.

13   Although the rulings of the Council of Trent (see note 5 above) do not explicitly require a sacred image to reproduce exactly what is written in the text which inspired it, the most widespread response was to give the closest

attention to every detail of the text. This problem generated a good deal of controversy and gave rise to more than one case brought by the Inquisition, including that involving Veronese. Of those described as 'moralist theorists of the Counter-Reformation', Cardinal Gabriele Paleotti comes closest to the thesis of literality. The second book of his *Discorso intorno alle imagini sacre e profane* narrowly restricts any imaginative licence or decontextualization on the part of the painter. However, Giovanni Andrea Gilio is one of a number of writers who took a more accommodating stance, and this tolerance also had its adherents in Spain, such as Vicente Carducho. On the situation in Spain, see Cristina Cañedo Argüelles, *Arte y teoría: la Contrarreforma en España,* Oviedo, 1982, and Palma Martínez-Burgos, *Idolos e imágenes. La controversia del arte religioso en el siglo XVI español,* Valladolid, 1990.

14   See Manuel Gómez Moreno, *El entierro del Conde de Orgaz,* Barcelona, 1943, p. 15. Also Annie Cloulas, *Greco*, Paris, 1993 pp. 80f., who provides several contemporary prices as references. For disputed valuations of the painting and other details, see San Román, *op. cit.*, pp. 142–55.

15   El Greco accepted the Council's decree, dated 30 May 1588, ordering the church of Santo Tomé to pay the 1,200 ducats of the first valuation and exonerated it from paying the extra 400 ducats added by the second valuation, but only after appealing to the authority of the Pope 'because', he declared, 'he had suffered [*por aber recibido agravio*] by freely giving the said 400 ducats to the said church and its priest and master of works'.

16   See Julián Gállego, *El pintor de artesano a artista,* Granada, 1976, ch. VIII, 'Los pleitos del Greco', pp. 101–18.

17   Antonio Palomino, *Museo Pictórico y Escala Óptica*, Madrid, 1947, p. 161.

18   On the subject of tax litigation and its legal and economic repercussions in Spain, see also Gállego, *op. cit.* (note 16 above); Pío Ballesteros, 'Los pintores ante el Fisco', *Revista de la Facultad de Derecho*, Madrid, 1942, p. 87; Francisco Calvo Serraller, *Teoría de la pintura del Siglo de Oro*, Madrid, 1981; Antonio Matilla, 'Comercio de pintura y alcabalas', *Goya*, no. 178, 1984, p. 180; Juan José Martín González, *El artista en la sociedad española del siglo XVII*, Madrid, 1984.

19   Documentation relating to the case of the *Espolio* can be found in M.R. Zarco del Valle, 'Documentos inéditos para la historia de las bellas artes en España', *Colección de documentos inéditos para la historia de España*, vol. 45, Madrid, 1870, pp. 591–613. See also Ángel López-Amo, 'Estudios de los contratos de obra artística de la catedral de Toledo en el siglo XVI', *Anuario del Derecho Español*, 1948–49, p. 103.

20   E. Lafuente Ferrari, 'Borrascas de la pintura y triunfos de su excelencia', *Archivo Español de Arte*, no. 61, 1944, pp. 77–103.

21   This in essence is the line of argument of all the Spanish writers of the period who took up this question: Gaspar Gutiérrez de los Ríos, Juan de Butrón, Francisco Pacheco, Jusepe Martínez, Calderón de la Barca, and other less prominent writers, including Palomino; Carducho's *Diálogos* include recollections written by various authorities who testified in the trial. These included such eminent figures as Lope de Vega, José de Valdivielso, Juan de Jáuregui, Lorenzo Vaderhamen, Juan Rodríguez de León, and Butrón himself, who acted for the plaintiff. An interesting point of comparison is supplied by Elena Favoro, *L'arte dei pittori in Venezia e i suoi statuti*, Florence, 1975.

22   See note 19.

23   See note 15.

24   See Palomino, *Museo, op. cit.*, pp. 841f.: 'And all the masters of this art therefore owe immortal thanks to Dominico Greco because he was the first to take up this fight in defence of the immunity of our art from sales tax; and all other court verdicts were based on that precedent; for this reason it is said that El Greco did not wish to sell his paintings but would pledge them while the tax suit lasted, because the sales tax was levied only on what was sold; if one does not sell, no tax can fall due.'

25   There are two inventories: the first was drawn up by El Greco's son Jorge Manuel in 1614, between 12 April and 7 July. The second, dated 7 August 1621, was also carried out by Jorge Manuel, on the occasion of his impending second marriage. See San Román, *El Greco en Toledo, op. cit.*, pp. 185–95. In both these inventories a disparity is evident between the large number of paintings and books and the scarcity of furnishings, which has led many writers to suppose that at the time of his death El Greco was on the verge of poverty. We should not forget that J. Martínez accused him of profligacy. However, as Wethey points out, there are no grounds for certainty here, since Jorge Manuel does not seem to have been particularly exact when recording goods other than books or paintings.

26   In his articles, 'The Toledo of El Greco' and 'Toledo and the Counter-Reformation' (see *El Greco of Toledo*, Toledo, Ohio, 1982, pp. 53–61), Richard L. Kagan demonstrates the importance of the honorifically titled see of the Primate of Spain, both in terms of the number of its members and of the extent of its influence. In particular, he analyses the crucial role as a driving force of the Counter-Reformation played by Gaspar de Quiroga, incumbent of the archbishopric between 1577 and 1594. It is noteworthy, moreover, that these dates coincide with the time of El Greco's arrival in the imperial city which he was to make his home. Quiroga's initiative was furthermore continued by his apostolic successors, in particular by Bernardo Sandoval y Rojas, who held the position from 1599. The new Tridentine

doctrine, as Kagan explains, returned again and again to the question of the control of images. Given the vehemence and strictness with which the new ethic was applied, and the fact that El Greco's clientele consisted almost entirely of religious foundations, it is hardly surprising that his Toledan works offer a perfect illustration of the religious and moral ideals of the Counter-Reformation, particularly with reference to the representation of the saints as intercessors, the glorification of the Virgin Mary, the doctrine of the Immaculate Conception and the exaltation of good works and penitence, as J. Brown notes ('El Greco as an artist of the Counter-Reformation' in *ibid.*, pp. 113 and 116).

The ideas of the Council of Trent are clearly reflected here. See in this connection the classic studies of Charles Dechob, *De l'influence du Concile de Trente sur la littérature et les beaux-arts chez les peuples catholiques*, Paris, 1884; Werner Weisbach, *El barroco como arte de la contrarreforma* (Spanish edition by E. Lafuente Ferrari), Madrid 1948; Emile Mâle, *L'art religieux de la fin du XVIe siècle, du XVIIe siècle et du XVIIIe siècle. Etude sur l'iconographie après la Concile de Trente. Italie, France, Espagne, Flandre*, Paris, 1947; Federico Zeri, *Pittura e Controriforma. Alle origini dell' "arte senza tempo"*, Turin, 1957; Romeo de Maio, *Michelangelo e la Controriforma*, Rome and Bari, 1978; María Calí *Da Michelangelo all'Escorial. Momenti del dibattito religioso nell'arte del Cinquecento*, Turin, 1980.

On the huge impact of the Council of Trent on local art, in addition to the studies cited above (see note 13) the following are also to be recommended: Julián Gállego, *Visión y símbolos en la pintura española del Siglo de Oro*, Madrid, 1972; Pilar Dávila, *Los sermones y el arte*, Valladolid, 1980; Santiago Sebastián, *Contrarreforma y barroco. Lecturas iconográficas e iconológicas*, Madrid, 1981; Ana María Roteta, *La ilustración del libro en la España de la Contrarreforma. Grabados de Pedro Ángel y Diego de Astor (1588–1636)*, Madrid, 1981; José Luis Bouza, *Religiosidad contrarreformista y cultura simbólica del barroco*, Madrid, 1990.

On the theme of Counter-Reformation inspiration in El Greco, although this is indubitably present in his treatment of religious themes, nevertheless we cannot dissent from the view expressed by Fernando Marías ('A propósito del manierismo y el arte español del siglo XVI' in John Shearman, *Manierismo*, Madrid, 1984, p. 37): 'In short we encounter here the religious painting of a Mannerist artist on orthodox Counter-Reformation themes, and not works of the *Contramaniera*, in which the desire for subjective form takes over from the lucid, decorous, emotive and devotional expression of a sacred theme from which any impropriety is absent. It was his emphasis on the formal which in the final analysis pointed El Greco's artistic situation towards the concrete rather than the abstract.'

27 For example, his response to accusations of 'great indecency' in the painting of the retable of the hospital of Illescas because it depicted two 'figures and faces of notable and well-known personages of the said city of Toledo wearing wheel ruffs', was that 'it is indeed a cause for wonderment when customs that are common throughout Christendom in that place are thought to be indecent' (see San Román, 'De la vida del Greco', *Archivo Español de Arte y Arqueología*, 3, 1927, pp. 139ff.).

28 Vicente Carducho, *Diálogos de la Pintura* (1633), ed. F. Calvo Serraller, Madrid, 1979, p. 344.

29 *Ibid.*, p. 345.

30 *Ibid.*, pp. 342f.: 'I praise pious zeal, but I must explain my understanding of this matter. The painting of religious subjects has two aspects. The first and most important is the essential sacred event or action ...: nothing of this can or should be altered or changed because this event is true and sacred. The second concerns the way something happened, or its circumstances; even during the lifetime of Christ mystery surrounded the main events and actions, accounts of these being based on incidental details, and these circumstances may be altered in painting, especially in order to achieve a particular purpose; as long as this does not alter the event or action fundamentally, or cause any indecency or impiety, but rather magnifies and better proclaims the mystery, thought or story, and inspires and communicates the situation more fully (through ways and customs of the region and of the time of the painting), it is praiseworthy to make choices aided by gravity and prudence, and with greater freedom when such circumstances do not conflict in any way with what is written in Scripture: and not only do I not believe it culpable, but I praise it as an act of wisdom to elaborate and explicate the essence of the story by presenting it through circumstances and details that are as appropriate and as decent as possible, and serious, because this promotes understanding and the worshiping of sacred events and acts, and former circumstances and old ways are not customary today and would not cause people to worship, and so it is necessary to substitute others ... for this reason Painting has only to proclaim the essence of the event or action to everyone with as much clarity, reverence, decency and authority as possible, so as to speak to everyone in the language of their own country and time.... Many things happen every day which could not be explained except by using commonly understood terms, and this is as true of sacred events as of human actions, and thus I deem it appropriate to use such licence with all decorum and decency, as long as the essence of the mystery is unchanged, as has been said.'

31 Most studies highlight the development of El Greco's career at the time of *The Burial of the Count of Orgaz*, and more generally during the 1580s and part of the 1590s. As if aware of a change in taste away from Mannerism, he seems at this time to force himself to a degree of compromise with an incipient naturalism which he subsequently completely broke away from.

32 Fray José de Sigüenza, *La fundación del Monasterio de El Escorial*, Madrid, 1963, p. 385.

33 See A.E. Pérez Sánchez, 'La crisis de la pintura española en torno a 1600', *España en las crisis del arte europeo*, Madrid, 1968, pp. 167–77; F. Calvo Serraller, 'La doctrina artística de Carducho entre el manierismo y el barroco: la teoría de la restitución', *Ponencias y comunicaciones del III Congreso Español de Historia del Arte*, Seville, 1980; and 'El problema del naturalismo en la crítica artística del Siglo de Oro', *Cuenta y Razón*, no. 7, 1982, pp. 83-99.

34 See Pérez Sánchez, *op. cit.*, p. 170: 'Juan Fernández Navarrete, who died in 1578, was perhaps the first to call for a move towards realism, with Venice as a model. Even before the Tuscan reformers, he was the first to bring about the synthesis of seen truth and felt emotion which became the mark of the Baroque. He died young and his work, a foretaste of later developments, was somewhat lost to sight, since no followers of his are known. It was the following generation, born around 1565–75 and reaching maturity around 1600, that best represented the situation of crisis to which we refer, experienced in a way that is almost moving by some of our artists....'

35 Sigüenza, *op. cit.*, p. 384.

36 *Ibid.*, p. 265.

37 As in Barrès, for example, who substitutes Arab for Byzantine: 'A masterpiece at once Arab and Catholic in feeling.'

38 See H.E. Wethey, *El Greco and his School*, Princeton, 1962, vol. I, pp. 67–69.

39 M. Gómez Moreno, *El Entierro, op. cit.*, p. 15.

40 Cossío was the first to emphasize this point, *op. cit.*, p. 110.

41 See E. Spina Barelli, *Teorici e scrittori d'arte tra manierismo e barocco*, Milan, 1966; Carlo Ossola, *Autunno del rinascimento. 'Idea del Tempio' dell'arte nell'ultimo Cinquecento*, Florence, 1971; Carmine Benincasa, *Sul manierismo come dentro a uno specchio*, Rome, 1979; Esther Nyholm, *Arte e teoria del Manierismo. II: Idea*, Odense, 1982.

42 Found by Xavier de Salas ('Un exemplaire des Vies de Vasari annoté par le Greco', *Gazette des Beaux-Arts*, 6th series, 69, pp. 177–80), this copy of Vasari bears annotations by Zuccaro and Tristán as well as those of El Greco. Like the autograph notes found some years later by Marías and Bustamante, this time in a copy of the 1556 Venetian edition of Vitruvius, with a commentary by Barbaro (*Las ideas artísticas de El Greco*, Madrid, 1981), these notes were to stimulate important attempts towards a deeper understanding of El Greco's thinking on art, a thinking clearly rooted in Neoplatonism as mediated by Michelangelo. We are fortunate today in having access to El Greco's notes on

Vasari, published together with various relevant studies by Xavier de Salas and an introduction by Fernando Marías: *El Greco y el arte de su tiempo. Las notas de El Greco a Vasari*, Madrid, 1992.

43 Gómez Moreno, *op. cit.*, p. 15.

44 As in his repeated and almost passionate defence of Michelangelo's famous saying: 'measurement must be in the eye'; El Greco's marginal note reads: 'And he knew best how to do this and no one could vie with him' [*Y lo mejor que sabía hacer ero esto y sin comparación*].

45 A great deal has been written, much of it contradictory, about the influence which Spanish culture may have exerted on El Greco's artistic development. Even today there is still little agreement: thus, for example, for Marías and Bustamante (*Las ideas, op. cit.*, pp. 218f.) his late 'extravagant' manner has much more to do with the coherent logic of his personal stylistic development than with contemporary Spanish spirituality.

46 See H.E. Wethey, *op. cit.*, p. 56.

47 Cossío, *El Greco, op. cit.*, p. 118.

48 According to Wethey (vol. II, p. 80), with reference to the *Entombment of Christ* of 1525, now in the Louvre.

49 Anthony Blunt, *Borromini*, London, 1979, p. 91.

50 Gómez Moreno, *op. cit.*, p. 21.

51 In fact, this is, nevertheless, in keeping with the ideas of El Greco, as has been shown by Marías and Bustamante (*op. cit.*, p. 145).

52 Cossío, *op. cit.*, pp. 119f.

53 See Moshe Barasch, *Light and Color in the Italian Renaissance Theory of Art*, New York, 1978.

54 In addition to the indubitable influence on the young Picasso, probably transmitted through the artistic coteries of Barcelona, the German Expressionists did the most to make use of and to communicate El Greco's artistic merit. The *Spanische Reise* of Julius Meier-Graefe certainly contributed to this, as did Hugo von Tschudi, culminating in an impassioned article by Franz Marc in the *Almanac* of the Blaue Reiter movement, which also established a line of descent between El Greco and Cézanne. German art historians, then closer to avant-garde movements, were soon involved in the rehabilitation of El Greco. The ground-breaking contribution made by the historian Dvořák has been acknowledged by J. Brown; an important connection (which cannot be explored here but should not be overlooked) also existed between this movement and Wilhelm Worringer, founder of the psychological history of art and an important ally of the German Expressionists. He also made the connection between these artists and various late Gothic phenomena.

55 G.C. Argan, *Borromini*, Milan, 1952, p. 43.

56 First articulated by Cossío, this point has been repeated in all subsequent studies of the *Burial*. However, in 'The Burial of the Count of Orgaz by El Greco', Sarah Schroth focuses on the funeral liturgy (in Brown, *Figures of Thought: El Greco as Interpreter of History, Tradition, and Ideas*, Washington, 1982).

57 A. Neumeyer, *El entierro del conde de Orgaz*, Madrid, 1981, p. 12.

58 Gómez Moreno, *op. cit.*, pp. 24f.

59 Cossío goes so far as to see the portraits in the *Burial* as prefiguring the later achievement of Velázquez himself.

60 This is a typical Mannerist feature, but the surprising aspect of El Greco's interpretation of this approach is the 'humanization' of the supernatural phenomenon. Not only are St Stephen and St Augustine without haloes or any of the usual luminous mandorlas used to identify superhuman beings, but they also seem to be fully integrated in the funeral ceremony taking place, just like a real bishop and deacon. This is in effect a departure from the spirit of contradiction characteristic of conventional Mannerism, the supernatural and the natural here being integrated in the same natural way. Certain unrealistic elements nevertheless remain, such as the physical improbability of the weightless appearance of a man in full armour, supported at the heaviest part of his body by an old man. Similarly, the incongruity of a bishop performing the function of lowering the body into the tomb is patent, even though the deceased is a high-ranking noble. This latter detail, however, conforms with Counter-Reformation teachings calling for a human aspect to be imparted to saintliness.

61 Antonio Covarrubias y Leiva, son of the architect Alonso de Covarrubias, was schoolmaster at the cathedral and a well-known local scholar. Two portraits of him by El Greco survive. One, signed and probably dating from around 1600, is in the Louvre, and the other, also signed, is in the El Greco museum in Toledo. The date of the latter is less certain.

62 This identification is much more controversial; the old man's face has also been ascribed to El Greco's brother Manusso, as well as to Andrés Núñez, the parish priest, but the most likely subject is Diego Covarrubias, older brother of Antonio. As bishop of Segovia and one of the theologians elected as deponent to the Council of Trent, in addition to his position as president of the Queen's Council of Castille, he attained the highest ecclesiastical and secular rank. He died in 1577, which means that, if this is indeed his portrait, it must have been painted from memory or with the aid of another portrait. Diego de Covarrubias was also painted on another occasion by El Greco; this portrait is now in the El Greco museum in Toledo, although it must be pointed out that some experts consider it to be not entirely authentic.

63 Gómez Martínez (*op. cit.*, p. 18) relies on a likeness between this figure and the portrait of Andrés Núñez now in the Segovian town of Martín Muñoz de las Posadas, where it was taken after being removed from the church at Navalperal. However, this supposed likeness is questionable; the painting is heavily retouched and, according to Wethey, is at best a copy after a lost original by El Greco.

64 This youthful figure forcibly attracts our attention, partly because, with the obvious exception of the boy kneeling in the foreground, he is the only lay figure without a beard, but also because, as befits his age, he seems untouched by the gravity of the situation and as if absorbed in his own, obviously worldly, everyday preoccupations. Placed at the very centre of the composition, this vacant, day-dreaming attitude plays a very effective role as an element of emotional *contrapposto*. Here we must recognize yet another feature of Mannerism, where, as Freedberg notes, figures tend to be all the same size, placed in a line which militates against any illusion of depth, and differentiated only by their faces. Even their expressions are often attenuated by the close conjunction of the heads or because they share a collective emotion. What is curious in the case of the figure under discussion is that we need to look a second time to become aware of the jarring lack of seriousness displayed by this youth, while the emotional unity of the totality nevertheless remains unbroken.

65 Of Francisco de Pisa we know that he was born in Toledo on 12 August 1534 and died at the age of 82 in the same city on 3 December 1616. Famous not only as the historian of his city, he was also a Doctor of Canonical Law, a professor of Holy Scripture, and dean of the faculties of Theology and Liberal Arts at the college of Santa Catalina.

66 Cossío, *op. cit.*, p. 131. In a note on this topic in his critical edition of the *Apuntamientos para la segunda parte de la 'Descripción de la Imperial Ciudad de Toledo'* by Francisco de Pisa (Toledo, 1976, p. 68), José Gómez-Menor suggests that Alvar Gómez de Castro, who composed the epitaph, must also be portrayed, although without establishing which figure might represent him.

67 This unproven but otherwise attractive suggestion is consistent with the residence of Cervantes in the city at this period and also fits Cossío's thesis that the *Burial* can be explained by means of a comparison with *Don Quixote*. This argument was subsequently given international exposure in the last chapter of Max Dvořák's famous *Kunstgeschichte als Geistesgeschichte* (1924). Entitled 'On El Greco and Mannerism', this chapter focuses particularly on *The Burial of the Count of Orgaz,* and Dvořák concludes by comparing the pure idealism of Don Quixote with El Greco's anti-materialist response.

68 The thematic elements of El Greco's painting of heaven conform completely with Tridentine doctrine. In the classic work by the Italian Dominican Antonio Polti, *Acerca de la Suprema Felicidad en el cielo* (1575), heaven is described as inhabited by innumerable hosts of angels and

saints in a rigidly pre-ordained hierarchical order. The unique role of the Virgin and the purifying aspect of childhood are given particular emphasis. See Colleen McDannell and Bernhard Lang, *Heaven, a History*, Yale, 1988, pp. 158ff.

69 Like similar speculations, however, this hypothesis has not found adherents.

70 Gómez Moreno, *op. cit.*, p. 23. This identification is also unfounded, being based on an 'apparent likeness'.

71 A. Neumeyer, *op. cit.*, p. 16.

72 The Mannerist character of the work has never been disputed, whether considered as a whole or analysed in its constituent elements. There has, moreover, been general agreement about the uncanny and quite exceptional formal and cultural synthesis El Greco succeeded in bringing to this masterpiece. The work's complex genealogy, apparent in its many debts to other artists – as in the similarity between the group formed by the saints and the Lord of Orgaz and certain works by Titian, whose brilliant palette is also discernible in the resplendent vestments of St Stephen and St Augustine, a detail which reminds some writers of the gold light of the Byzantine, while others recall Tintoretto's skies, Michelangelo's figures, and so on – is a sign of the maturity of El Greco's genius; he succeeded in giving unity and a complete organic meaning to the whole.

73 Juan de Butrón, *Discursos apologéticos en los que se defiende la ingenuidad de la Pintura* (Madrid, 1626), in F. Calvo Serraller, *Teoría de la pintura del Siglo de Oro, op. cit.*, p. 218. Also of interest is Butrón's reference to El Greco in his report to the Consejo Real de Hacienda, 'Por los pintores y su exempción', in the *Memorial informatorio por los pintores en el pleito que tratan con el señor Fiscal de su Magestad, en el Real Consejo de Hazienda*, published as an appendix to the *Diálogos de la Pintura* by Vicente Carducho, Madrid, 1633, fol. 216 *verso* and 217 *recto*: 'In accordance with the agreements of the Real Consejo de Hazienda concerning Painters: that as it has been determined that sales tax is not to be levied on paintings in its possession, this was decreed, that Dominico el Griego be absolved from the demand which had been made of him for sales tax on the retable which he made for the church of Our Lady at Illescas, according to the precedents presented by Painters in this case, all the evidence having been heard by the Council, it is declared that Painting is exempt.'

74 Given that both artists had come to Spain from Italy and that El Greco had died, Carducho's silence is inexplicable. It is true that he mentions few of his contemporary colleagues, apart from major figures and those with whom he was closely linked. However, the most natural explanation of his disregard of El Greco is to be found not only in the dissension between a painter who adhered to pure Mannerism and one who had developed beyond it, but in the even deeper divide between an orthodox Tuscan artist and one trained in Venice, who dared to deny the primacy of drawing and even on occasion went so far as to mock Michelangelo, Vasari and other idols still venerated by Carducho, the Florentine artist who had made his home in Spain.

75 Pacheco visited El Greco in Toledo in 1611 and in fact refers to him several times in his treatise. See F. Pacheco, *Arte de la Pintura* (Seville, 1649), ed. B. Bassegoda i Hugas, Madrid, 1990, p. 349: 'I asked Dominico Greco in the year 1611, which was more difficult, drawing or colour? and he replied that it was colour. And nothing is as amazing as to hear him speak with such little regard for Michelangelo – who was the father of painting – saying that he was a good man who did not know how to paint ...'; p. 404: 'And we may even count among these El Greco because, although we wrote elsewhere against some opinions and paradoxes of his, we cannot exclude him from the great painters, for we see some works by his hand so striking and vivid (in that style of his) that they equal the art of the greatest'; p. 415: 'and in Spain there are those who have thought to praise a particular way of painting with smudges not adopted then nor later imitated by anyone'; p. 440f.: 'Dominico Greco showed me in the year 1611 a store of clay models he used in his works and, what was beyond all admiration, the originals of all the paintings he had ever painted in oil on smaller canvases in a room he told his son to show me. What would the vain and the lazy say to this? Would they not fall dead on hearing this example? Would those pygmies still pride themselves on their skill and talent on seeing this diligence of the giants? I have even seen and known some who start their works in wet oil without plans, drawings or cartoons'; p. 483: 'who would believe that Dominico Greco took his paintings in hand many times and retouched them over and over again to make the colours more distinct and striking and to give those violent marks feigning mastery? I call this working hard for a poor result.'; p. 537: 'Dominico Greco, who was a great philosopher of acute sayings and who wrote on painting, sculpture and architecture'; p. 698: 'but let us give this glory to Dominico Greco because he adhered most closely to the texts: although when I saw him he was poorly dressed in the rough serge of a recluse, such was not his way of life, as we shall see.'

76 Pacheco, *op. cit.*, p. 441.

77 J. Martínez, *Discursos praticables del nobilísimo arte de la Pintura* (Saragossa, 1673?), ed. V. Carderera, Madrid, 1866, pp. 183f.: 'At that time there came from Italy a painter called Dominico Greco; he was said to be a disciple of Titian. He settled in the famous and ancient city of Toledo. He introduced such an extravagant style that to this day nothing has been seen to equal its capriciousness; attempting to discuss it would bring confusion even to the soundest minds, his works being so dissimilar that they do not seem to be by the same hand. He came to this city with great credit, so much so that it was said that there was nothing superior to his works; and in truth he executed some works which are worthy of estimation and which can be put with those of famous painters; his way of life was as extravagant as his painting; it is not known with certainty what he did with his works, as he used to say no price was high enough for them and so he gave them in pledge to his patrons, who willingly advanced him what he asked; he earned many ducats, but spent them in too much ostentatious display in his house, even keeping paid musicians so that he could enjoy every delight while eating. His works were many, but the only wealth he left were 200 unfinished paintings by his hand; he reached an advanced age, always enjoying great fame. He was a famous architect and very eloquent in his discourse; he had few pupils, as none cared to follow his capricious and extravagant style, which was suited only to himself. With this example in mind, our student should turn to the real and true path and follow many different artists both ancient and modern, for although this way led him to fortune, anyone who imitated him would put himself in jeopardy and would not succeed with it.'

78 José García Hidalgo, *Principios para estudiar el nobilísimo y real Arte de la Pintura* (Madrid, 1693), Madrid, 1965 edition, fol. 8 *verso*: 'Also El Greco, it seems, despite his great study of anatomy, was obliged to pursue a most disagreeable and outrageous style; for it is true that each must work with his own nature.'

79 See above, notes 17 and 24. Palomino, *op. cit.*, pp. 840–43.

80 Palomino (p. 840) makes the following comments concerning the *Burial*: 'But above all he is praised for the picture of the Burial of the Count of Orgaz ... and El Greco pledged the said painting for 2,000 ducats, for reasons I will explain later; and although this may be a digression, I will not omit to mention that this painting was commissioned in the year 1584 by His Eminence Lord Don Gaspar de Quiroga, Cardinal Archbishop of Toledo, at the request of the priests of the said parish ... and in the Jesuit house in the same city there is another painting also by his hand and of the same theme, but without the Glory above ... and in truth both paintings look as if they had been painted by Titian'; and further on, p. 841: 'But, seeing that his paintings were mistaken for those of Titian, he endeavoured to change his style – with such extravagance that he succeeded only in making his painting derisory and ridiculous, as much for its disjointed drawing as for the harshness of the colours.'

81 As, for example, Ceán (*Diccionario histórico de los más ilustres profesores de las Bellas Artes en España*, Madrid, 1800, vol. V, p. 5) states of the

painting of St Maurice: 'This picture is harsh, disagreeable, extravagant and in what is known as his second style, when it should belong to the first, given those who commissioned it and the place for which it was painted. It is said that he adopted this style to differentiate himself from Titian, whom he resembled when he painted carefully and thoughtfully; but this is just one of many tall stories recounted about this artist.' Llaguno reiterates this comment in his *Noticias de los arquitectos y arquitectura en España desde su restauración*, Madrid, 1829, vol. III, pp. 137f.: 'It was said that he had been a disciple of Titian. He practised the three arts of painting, sculpture and architecture, and made himself famous for the extravagance of his style in the first two. The explanation given for this extravagance is that, his paintings being mistaken for those of his master Titian, he did not wish to be confused with anyone and changed his style completely. I imagine that this change did not take place, but that his style had always been arid and confused and some of his pictures, made with much study and consideration, came out well while those he made in a hurry were bad or even abominable.'

82 See the detailed transcriptions in the excellent anthology of opinions on this topic assembled by José Álvarez Lopera, *De Céan a Cossío: la fortuna crítica del Greco en el siglo XIX*, Madrid, 1987.

83 Céan himself (see above), in his commentary on the *Burial*, praises only the magnificent portraits of the lower section, a recurrent theme among Spanish critics throughout the greater part of the nineteenth century.

84 Manet, in a letter to Zacharie Astruc dated 17 September 1865 (Edouard Manet, *Voyage en Espagne*, ed. Juliet Wilson-Bareau, Paris, 1988, pp. 49f.), writes as follows: 'Only two men in that country, apart from the Master (Velázquez), attracted me: Greco, whose work is strange, although his portraits are extremely beautiful ... and Goya.' Edmond Bazire, *Manet*, 1884 (*Manet raconté par lui-même et par ses amis*, Geneva, 1953, vol. I, p. 95), records that 'he was struck by the Spanish', while Thoré, in a review published in the *Indépendent belge*, 15 June 1864 (*ibid.*, I, pp. 112f.), declared: 'However, it is El Greco, the pupil of Titian and the teacher of Velázquez, that M. Manet's *Christ* resembles.' To this Baudelaire replied with a letter telling the critic that what he called *pastiches* were merely chance similarities (*ibid.*, pp. 112f.). Degas, for his part, became a collector of works by El Greco. See note 54.

85 Zuloaga came to possess an important collection of works by El Greco, and the influence of the latter on the former is obvious. It seems to have been he who transmitted this interest to Rilke as well as to compatriots such as Rusiñol, who became one of the principal champions of the then unknown painter, defending him in the journal *Luz*, buying works for the museum of Sitges and organizing a national celebration which included erecting a statue of the artist,

unveiled in the spring of 1898. It is also clear that Picasso was infected by this enthusiasm in Barcelona, as was also the case with other Spanish artists who formed part of the vibrant Catalan artistic scene. However, in addition to these obvious points of reference, El Greco's renown among Spanish painters at the end of the century was much more widespread and affected artists as diverse as Julio Romero de Torres and José Gutiérrez Solana, to cite only the two most opposite poles. His rehabilitation followed the same lines as the re-establishment of Goya's reputation in Spain, being championed by artists long before critics and art historians. However, decades were still to pass before El Greco became genuinely popular in Spain, despite the formidable campaign mounted by this group of initiates.

86 Pérez Galdós, in an article written in 1870 ('Las generaciones artísticas en la ciudad de Toledo' in *Obras completas*, Madrid, 1973, vol. III, pp. 1344–78), reiterates a number of commonplaces about El Greco, although this does not prevent him from ascribing to him 'the perception of a strange ideal', or from recognizing the *Burial* as his masterpiece. It is also true that the protagonist of his novel *Ángel Guerra* seems to have stepped out of a painting by El Greco; clearly his works were very much in the author's mind during the writing of this novel. Emilia Pardo Bazán had closer personal links with contemporary painters and even wrote a novel, *La Quimera*, whose protagonist was based on them. He has little that is new to say about El Greco, however, even though he was writing a quarter of a century after Galdós. Nevertheless, he does reflect the critical evolution taking place at the time, by which El Greco's 'strange ideal' and 'monomania' became an 'ardent asceticism', 'the sublime dreams of a colourist', and the 'ecstasy of the faithful', qualities which ultimately came to enjoy a 'mysterious prestige' ('Sobre la blanca Sitjes. Carta a Domenico Theotocopuli, llamado el Greco', *La Vanguardia*, Barcelona, 23 July 1895).

87 The support of the Generation of 98 was virtually unanimous: Azorín, Unamuno, Baroja, Ganivet and Maeztu not only put El Greco on the same level as Velázquez but also saw in him the spiritual reflection of the soul of Castilian Spain, a topic of fundamental concern to all the members of this circle. See Álvarez Lopera, *op. cit.*, pp. 89–101.

88 The rise of art history in Spain cannot be understood in its scientific and academic aspects without taking into account the contribution of the Institución Libre de Enseñanza. Crucial to the rehabilitation of El Greco in Spain undertaken by its most prominent members, this involved the analysis of formal issues as well as of the Spanish cultural context. See J. Brown, 'El Greco, the man and the myths' in *El Greco of Toledo*, *op. cit.*, pp. 13–33, and Álvarez Lopera, *op. cit.*, pp. 79–101.

89 See above, notes 54, 84 and 85. Two distinct lines of argument were employed by the international avant-garde movements that championed the cause of El Greco. The first was propounded by the French Realists, Impressionists and Symbolists, and later led Spanish critics and art historians to identify El Greco as the forerunner of these schools, with no real grounds other than, perhaps, the obsession with affirmation from outside that, until quite recently, afflicted Spain throughout its long years of isolation. The second was advanced by the German Expressionists, in particular the members of the Blaue Reiter group, for whom El Greco was not only of intrinsic merit but also a real precedent. In this context, although the influence of El Greco on avant-garde artists of the twentieth century is beyond the scope of the present study, I cannot omit the important testimony of a contemporary Spanish painter firmly rooted in Expressionism, Luis Gordillo, who singled out works by El Greco from the treasures of the Prado (see Luis Gordillo, 'Desde el Greco' in *Doce artistas de vanguardia en el Museo del Prado*, Madrid, 1990, pp. 79–87).

90 A comment noted by Carl Justi, who dates it 1881, at the time of a visit to the Prado in the company of Madrazo (see 'Los comienzos del Greco' in *Estudios de arte español*, Madrid, n.d., vol. II, pp. 235–54).

91 Cossío, *op. cit.*, pp. 122–28.

92 Apart from the commonplace view that El Greco suffered from periods of temporary madness, in our own time many scholars and scientists have been fascinated by attempts to diagnose physical or psychological illness as explanations of the painter's peculiar style. From the Spanish ophthalmologist Germán Beritens, who launched the astigmatism hypothesis (*Aberraciones del Greco científicamente consideradas*, Madrid, 1913), to the Portuguese doctor Ricardo Jorge (*Nueva contribución biográfica, crítica y médica al estudio del pintor Domenico Theotocopuli*, Coimbra, 1913), who diagnosed paranoia, there has been an unceasing flow of such reductive interpretations, generally produced by writers with little knowledge of the history of painting. Even so reputable a figure as the great Spanish scientist and writer Gregorio Marañón stresses the pathological aspect in the otherwise useful discussion in his well-known article entitled *El Greco y Toledo* (Madrid, 1956), suggesting that his models may well have been taken from the city asylum.

93 Cossío, *op. cit.*, p. 259, note 4.

94 Gómez Moreno, *op. cit.*, p. 25.

95 Palomino, *op. cit.*, p. 840.

96 Catalogue number 830. In the 1920 catalogue of the museum it is described as a 'copy by Jorge Manuel retouched by his father's hand'. Wethey (*op. cit.*, vol. II, pp. 211f.) is of the same opinion. A smaller version (90 x 75 cm), once in the collection of Muñoz Ortiz, is now lost.

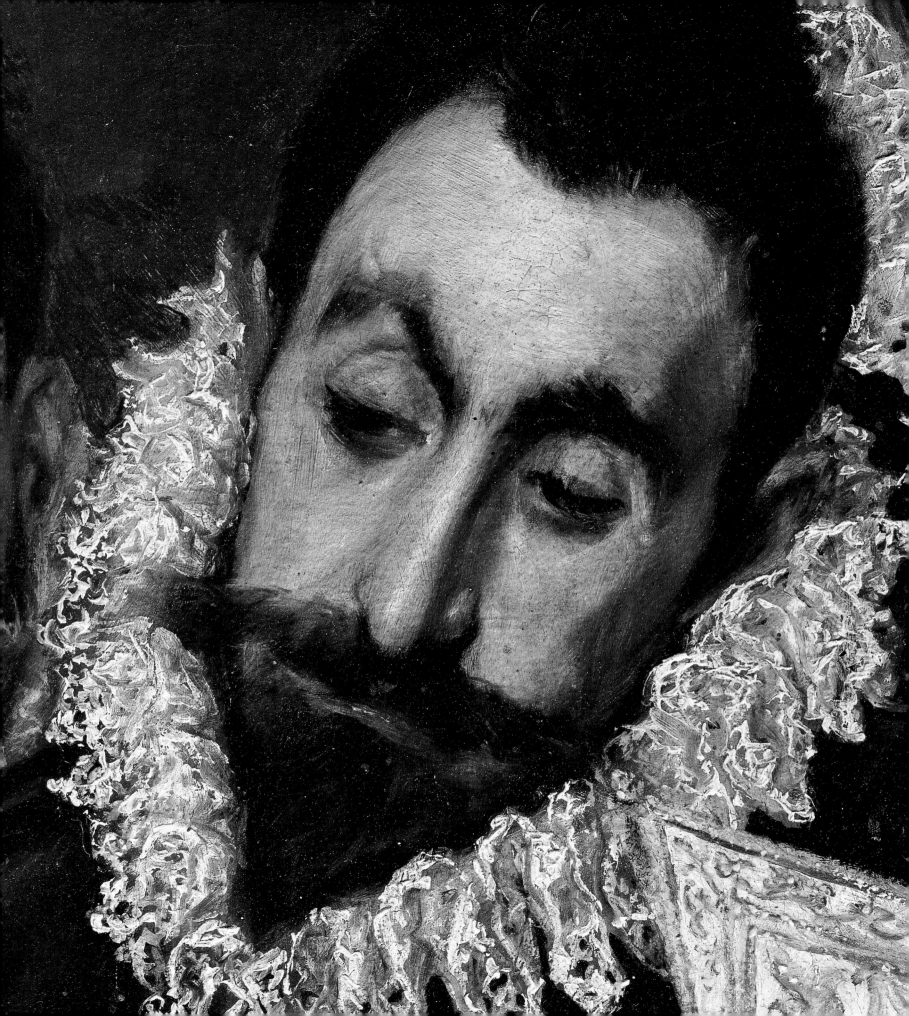

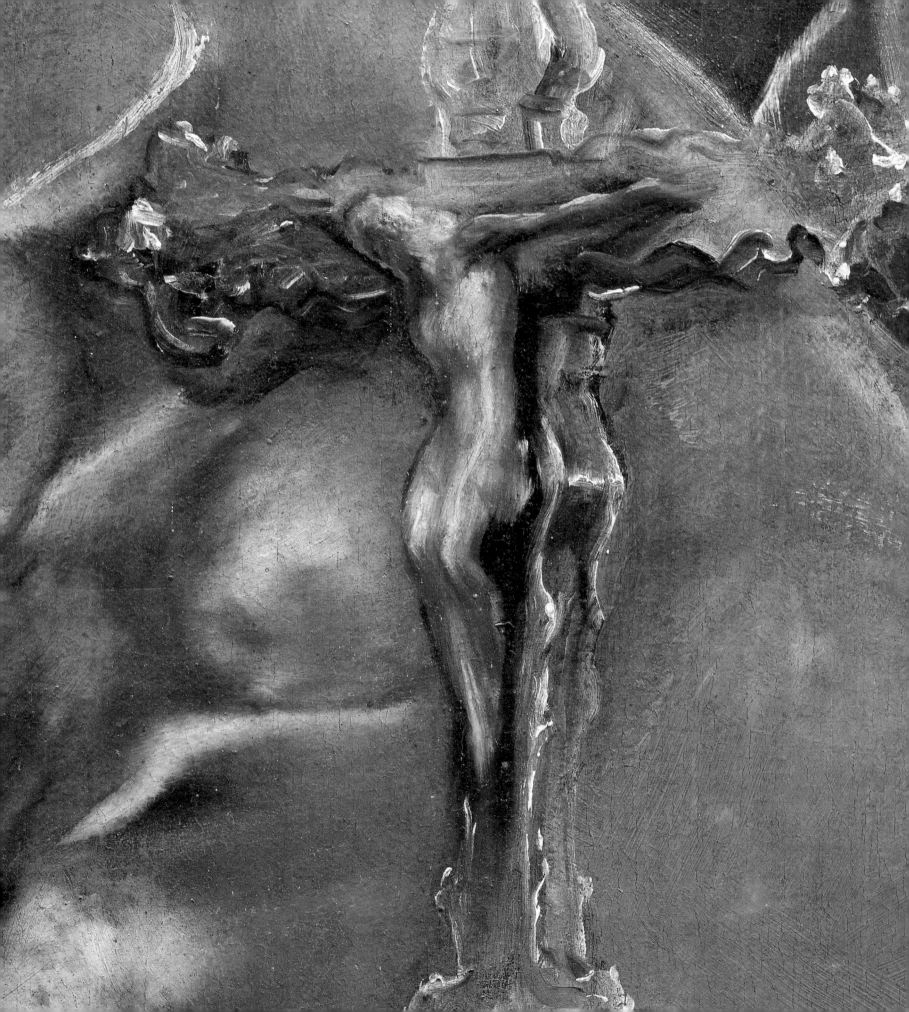

Select bibliography

1600–5 J. de Sigüenza, *Historia de la Orden de San Jerónimo*, Madrid.

1605 F. de Pisa, *Descripción de la Imperial Ciudad de Toledo*, Toledo. (The *Apuntamientos para la segunda parte de la 'Descripción…'*, remained in manuscript until their publication in 1976, Toledo).

1614 G. Mancini, *Considerazioni sulla Pittura* (ed. A. Marucchi and L. Salerno, Rome, 1956).

1649 F. Pacheco, *Arte de la Pintura*, Seville.

1673? J. Martínez, *Discursos practicables del nobilísimo arte de la pintura*, Saragossa. (First publication of the manuscript was by Mariano Nogués Secall in *El Diario Zaragozano*, 1853–54; subsequently edited by Valentín Carderera, Madrid, 1866; Julián Gállego, Barcelona, 1950, and Madrid, 1988).

1715–24 A. Palomino, *El Museo Pictórico, y Escala Óptica*, Madrid.

1772–94 A. Ponz, *Viaje de España*, 18 vols, Madrid.

1800 J.A. Ceán Bermúdez, *Diccionario histórico de los más ilustres profesores de las Bellas Artes en España*, Madrid.

1829 E. Llaguno y Amirola, *Noticias de los arquitectos y arquitectura de España desde su restauración*, Madrid.

1843 N. Magán, 'Galería de pinturas. Escuela Española (El entierro del Conde de Orgaz, cuadro del Greco)', *Semanario Pintoresco Español*, Madrid, year VIII (28 March), pp. 169–71.

1848 W. Stirling-Maxwell, *Annals of the Artists of Spain*, London.

1857 S. Ramón Parro, *Toledo en la mano*, Toledo.

1869 P. Lefort, 'Le Greco', *Histoire des peintres de toutes les écoles*, vol. 4: *École Espagnole*, Paris.

1870 M.R. Zarco del Valle, 'Documentos inéditos para la historia de las bellas artes en España', *Colección de documentos inéditos para la historia de España*, vol. 45, Madrid.

1876 J. Foradada y Castán, 'Datos biográficos desconocidos o mal apreciados, acerca del célebre pintor Dominico Theotocópoli', *Revista de Archivos, Bibliotecas y Museos*, 6, pp. 137ff.

1902 S. Sanpere y Miquel, 'Domenikos Theotokopuli El Greco', *Hispania*, Barcelona, no. 71 (30 January), pp. 26–49.
S. Viniegra, *Catálogo ilustrado de la exposición de las obras de Dominico Theotocópoli llamado El Greco*, Madrid.

1906 P. Lafond, 'Domenikos Theotokopuli dit Le Greco', *Les Arts*, no. 58 (October), pp. 1–32.

1908 M.B. Cossío, *El Greco*, Madrid.
C. Justi, 'Der Anfang des Greco', *Miscellaneen aus drei Jahrhunderten spanischen Kunstlebens*, Berlin.

1910 J. Meier-Graefe, *Spanische Reise*, Berlin.
F. de B. San Román, *El Greco en Toledo*, Toledo.

1911 J. Meier-Graefe, *El Greco*, Munich.

1912 M. Barrès, *Greco ou le secret de Tolède*, Paris.

1913 E. Bertaux, 'Notes sur le Greco. Le Byzantinisme', *Revue de l'art ancien et moderne*, 33.
K. Steinbart, 'Greco und die spanische Mystik', *Repertorium für Kunstwissenschaft*, 36, pp. 121–34.

1914 A. de Beruete y Moret, *El Greco, pintor de retratos*, Toledo.
H. Kehrer, *Die Kunst des Greco*, Munich.

1915 J.R. Mélida, 'El arte antiguo y El Greco', *Boletín de la Sociedad Española de Excursiones*, 23 (June), pp. 89–103.

1916 A.L. Mayer, *El Greco*, Munich.
M.R. Zarco del Valle, *Datos documentales para la historia del arte español*, vol. 2: *Documentos de la Catedral de Toledo*, Madrid.

1920 R. Ramírez de Arellano, *Catálogo de artífices que trabajaron en Toledo*, Toledo.

1924 M. Dvořák, *Kunstgeschichte als Geistesgeschichte. Studien zur Abendländischen Kunstentwicklung*, Munich.

1925 E. Du Gué Trapier, *El Greco*, New York.

1926–27 A. Vegué y Goldoni, 'En torno a la figura del Greco', *Arte Español*, 8, pp. 70–79.

1927 F. de B. San Román, *De la vida del Greco*, Madrid.
J.F. Willumsen, *La jeunesse du peintre El Greco*, Paris.

1928 U. Bottazzi, 'I libri del Greco', *Bolletino del Reale Istituto di Archeologia e Storia dell'Arte*, II.

1929 R. Byron, 'Greco. The Epilogue to Byzantine Culture', *The Burlington Magazine*, 55, no. 319 (October), pp. 160–76.
A.L. Mayer, 'El Greco – an Oriental Artist', *The Art Bulletin*, XI, 2.

1930 J. Pijoan, 'El Greco – a Spaniard', *The Art Bulletin*, XII, pp. 13–18.
E.K. Waterhouse, 'El Greco's Italian Period', *Art Studies*, 7, pp. 61–88.

1931 J. Cassou, *Le Greco*, Paris.
J. Zarco Cuevas, *Pintores españoles en San Lorenzo el Real de El Escorial (1566–1613)*, Madrid.

1932 A.M. Brizio, 'Il Greco a Venezia', *L'Arte*, XXXV.
A. Kyrou, *Domenikos Theotokopoulos*, Athens.

1937 D. Talbot Rice, 'El Greco and Byzantium', *The Burlington Magazine*, 70.

1938 L. Goldscheider, *El Greco*, Oxford and New York.
E. Harris, 'A Decorative Scheme by El Greco', *The Burlington Magazine*, 72, pp. 154–64.
M. Legendre and A. Hartmann, *El Greco*, Paris.

1939 C. Zervos, *Les oeuvres du Greco en Espagne*, Paris.

1939–40 A. Blunt, 'El Greco's Dream of Philip II: An Allegory of the Holy League', *Journal of the Warburg and Courtauld Institutes*, 3, pp. 58–69.

1940–41 X. de Salas, 'La valoración del Greco por los románticos franceses', *Archivo Español de Arte*, 14, pp. 397–406.
A.L. Mayer, 'Notas sobre la iconografía sagrada en las obras del Greco', *Archivo Español de Arte*, 14, pp. 164–68.

1943 M. Gómez Moreno, *Obras maestras del arte español. El entierro del Conde de Orgaz*, Barcelona.

J. López Rey, 'El Greco's Baroque Light and Form', *Gazette des Beaux-Arts*, 6th series, XXIV, pp. 73–88.

1948 N. Cossío de Jiménez, *El Greco. Notes on his Birthplace, Education and Family*, London.

1950 L. Bronstein, *El Greco*, New York.
J. Camón Aznar, *Dominico Greco*, Madrid.

1954 X. de Salas, 'Más valoraciones románticas del Greco', *Clavileño*, 5, pp. 19–31.
J.G. Lemoine, 'La luz en los cuadros del Greco', *Revista de Ideas Estéticas*, 45.
M.S. Soria, 'Greco's Italian Period', *Arte Veneta*, VIII, pp. 213–21.

1956 G. Marañón, *El Greco y Toledo*, Madrid.
H. Soehner, 'Der Stand der Greco-Forschung', *Zeitschrift für Kunstgeschichte*, 19, pp. 47–75.
A. Vallentin, *El Greco*, Buenos Aires.

1957 M. Florissone, 'La mystique plastique du Greco et les antécédents de son style', *Gazette des Beaux-Arts*, 2.
A. Neumeyer, *El Greco (Domenico Theotocopuli): Das Begräbnis des Grafen Orgaz. Einführung von…*, Stuttgart.
H. Soehner, 'Greco in Spanien', *Münchner Jahrbuch der Bildenden Kunst*, 3rd series, vol. 8, 1957, pp. 122–94; 9–10, 1958–59, pp. 147–242; 11, 1960, pp. 173–217.
R. Wittkower, 'El Greco's Language of Gesture', *Arts News*, 56, pp. 45ff.

1958 E. Du Gué Trapier, *El Greco. Early Years at Toledo*, New York.

1959 P. Guinard, *Greco*, Geneva.

1960 K. Ipser, *El Greco der Maler des Christlichen Weltbildes*, Brunswick.

1961 P. Kelemen, *El Greco revisited. Candia, Venice, and Toledo*, New York.
C.D. Mertzios, 'D. Theotocopoulos: nouveaux éléments biographiques', *Arte Veneta*, XV, pp. 217–19.
F.J. Sánchez Cantón, *El Greco*, Milan.

1962 H.E. Wethey, *El Greco and his School*, Princeton.

1963 P. Troutman, *El Greco*, London.

1964 H.E. Wethey, 'Michelangelo e El Greco', *Palatino*, VIII.

1966 A. Braham, 'Two Notes on Greco and Michelangelo', *The Burlington Magazine*, 108, no. 759 (June), pp. 307–8.
A. Emiliani, *El Greco*, Novara.

1967 L. Bronstein, *El Greco*, New York and London.
X. de Salas, 'Un exemplaire des Vies de Vasari annoté par le Greco', *Gazette des Beaux-Arts*, 6th series, 69, pp. 177–80.
X. de Salas, *Miguel Ángel y El Greco*, Madrid.
L. Puppi, *El Greco*, Florence.

1968 M.E. Gómez Moreno, *Catálogo de las pinturas del Museo del Greco en Toledo*, Madrid.
J. Guerrero Lovillo, 'Lo que España dio al Greco', *España en la crisis del arte europeo*, Madrid.
A.E. Pérez Sánchez, 'La crisis de la pintura española en torno a 1600', *España en la crisis del arte europeo*, Madrid.

1969 E. Lafuente Ferrari and J.M. Pita Andrade, *Il Greco di Toledo e il suo espressionismo estremo*, Milan.
G. Manzini and T. Frati, *L'opera completa del Greco*, Milan.

1972 D. Angulo Íñiguez and A.E. Pérez Sánchez, *Pintura toledana de la primera mitad del siglo XVII*, Madrid.

1973 D. Davies, 'The Influence of Philosophical and Theological Ideas on the Art of El Greco in Spain', *Actas del XXIII Congreso Internacional de Arte*, vol. 2, Granada, pp. 242–49.
J. Gudiol, *Doménikos Theotokopoulos El Greco 1541–1614*, New York.
J. Lassaigne, *El Greco*, Paris and London.

1975 M. Constantoudaki, 'Domenicos Théotocopoulos de Candie à Venise. Documents inédits (1566–1568)', *Thesaurimata*, 12, pp. 292–308.

1976 D. Davies, *El Greco*, Oxford and New York.

1978 R. De Maio, *Michelangelo e la Controriforma*, Rome and Bari.

1980 M. Cali, *Da Michelangelo all'Escorial. Momenti del dibattito religioso nell'arte del Cinquecento*, Turin.

1981 K. Baetjer, 'El Greco', *The Metropolitan Museum of Art Bulletin*, New York.
F. Marías and A. Bustamante, *Las ideas artísticas de El Greco*, Madrid.

1982 J. Brown (ed.), *Figures of Thought: El Greco as Interpreter of History, Tradition and Ideas*, Studies in the History of Art, 11, Washington, D.C.
J. Brown *et al.*, *El Greco of Toledo*, Toledo, Ohio.
A.E. Pérez Sánchez *et al.*, *El Toledo de El Greco*, Madrid.

1984 J. Brown (ed.), *El Greco: Italy and Spain*, Studies in the History of Art, 13, Washington, D.C.

1986 R.G. Mann, *El Greco and his Patrons. The Major Projects*, Cambridge.

1987 J. Álvarez Lopera, *El Greco: textos, documentos y bibliografía*, vol. II: De Ceán a Cossío: La fortuna crítica del Greco en el siglo XIX, Madrid.

1988 J.-L. Scefer, *Le Greco ou l'éveil des ressemblances*, Paris.

1990 Several authors, *El Greco of Crete*, Heraklion.

1991 F. Marías, *El Greco*, Madrid.

1992 X. de Salas and F. Marías, *El Greco y el arte de su tiempo. Las notas de El Greco a Vasari*, Madrid.

1993 A. Cloulas, *Greco*, Paris.
C.L. Ragghianti, *Periplo del Greco*, Milan.